Nkx

Critical Guides to French Texts

EDITED BY ROGER LITTLE, WOLFGANG VAN EMDEN, DAVID WILLIAMS

MOLIÈRE

L'Avare

Second edition

G. J. Mallinson

Fellow and Tutor in French,
Trinity College, Oxford

Grant & Cutler Ltd
1993

© Grant & Cutler Ltd 1993

ISBN 0 7293 0348 9

First edition 1988
Second edition 1993

I.S.B.N. 84-599-2541-2

DEPÓSITO LEGAL: V. 70-1993

Printed in Spain by
Artes Gráficas Soler, S.A., Valencia
for
GRANT & CUTLER LTD
55-57 GREAT MARLBOROUGH STREET, LONDON W1V 2AY

Contents

For Margaret

Note

All references to the text of *L'Avare* are to the edition of
Fernand Angué, published by Bordas in the series Univers des
Lettres. This has been chosen for its accessibility and because,
unlike most other critical editions, the lines are numbered
consecutively throughout. Quotations from all other works of
Molière are taken from the *Œuvres complètes*, edited by
G. Couton and published by Gallimard in the Bibliothèque de la
Pléiade. References to works listed in the Select Bibliography
take the following form: italicised number of the item in the
Bibliography, followed, where appropriate, by a page number.
Full bibliographical details of other works referred to are given
in the footnotes.

Introduction

. . . son excellent *Avare*,
Que ceux de l'esprit plus bizarre
Ont rencontré fort à leur goût
Du commencement jusqu'au bout.
(Robinet, *Lettre en vers*, 10.11.1668;
see *15*, I, p.321)

L'Avare is one of Molière's most popular comedies. In a table of statistics published for the tercentenary of the dramatist's death, it stood second only to *Tartuffe* in the number of performances given up to 1973 at the Comédie Française.[1] What lies behind the play's enduring appeal to readers and audiences is a matter of speculation, but the liveliness of its prose, the rich variety of its comic effects, the fascination exerted by the miser, whose unsocial attitudes and behaviour make him a compelling figure in all ages, must contribute in various ways to its lasting popularity. And yet for critics the comedy remains something of an enigma and has aroused a particularly wide range of responses. Many have viewed it as an acutely disturbing play in which the intensity of the miser's obsession, the fragile relationship of father and son or the artificiality of the ending all pose different problems. Goethe's assessment that the play is deeply tragic ('im hohen Sinne tragisch') recorded in his conversation with Eckermann of 12 May 1825,[2] has often been echoed in later commentaries, and, writing at the end of the last century, Sarcey was led to observe of the comedy that 'l'impression générale n'est point de gaieté franche' (*19*, II, p.130). In more recent times, critics have followed this same

---

[1] *L'Avare* had 2367 performances, and *Tartuffe* 3007. (The next three in order were *Le Médecin malgré lui* (2177), *Le Misanthrope* (2001) and *Le Malade imaginaire* (1887).) Figures compiled by Sylvie Chevalley in *Le Petit Molière, 1673-1973*, Paris: Authier, 1973.

[2] J.P. Eckermann, *Gespräche mit Goethe in den letzten Jahren seines Lebens*, F. Bergemann, Wiesbaden: Insel, 1955, p.142.

approach: Wilson sees in it so much that is 'essentially tragic' (*3*, p.xlvi) that he is led to question how far it may properly be termed a comedy, and Attinger unhesitatingly qualifies the work as 'dur' and 'démoralisant' (*21*, p.158). For audiences in the seventeenth century, however, the play provided delightful entertainment, a fact confirmed by an early review in Robinet's *Lettre en vers* (15.9.1668) which spoke of:

> Un *Avare* qui divertit,
> Non pas, certes, pour un petit,
> Mais au-delà de ce qu'on peut dire,
> Car, d'un bout à l'autre, il fait rire
> (see *15*, I, pp.318-19)

Certain critics since that time have been at pains to demonstrate that it can still make an audience laugh. For Eustis, *L'Avare* is 'one of Molière's funniest plays' (*24*, p.174) and, for McBride, Harpagon is 'la création la plus invinciblement comique et dense' in the dramatist's output (*45*, p.62). Indeed, some commentators have seen so much that is amusing in the comedy as to conclude that it is simply trivial and unsophisticated. For Fénelon (*13*, p.105), Molière set out merely to please 'les spectateurs les moins délicats', and the play has been seen by a more recent critic as just a loose sequence of comic sketches (*32*, p.86).

This diversity of critical opinion is reflected also in the range of interpretations recorded in the theatre. Leloir's performance at the Théâtre Français in 1880 has been described as 'un Avare sinistre, sombre, à la voix incisive et mordante' (*23*, p.144); Signoret was seen to create a 'visionnaire terrible' (*Comoedia*, 7.12.1929, see *23*, p.147), and the production of J.-P. Roussillon in 1969 appeared to one critic as an '*Avare* tragique'.[3] By contrast, in the 1890s, Coquelin *cadet* emphasised in his interpretation the mechanical monomania of Harpagon, conceiving the character as 'un agité, en proie à une idée fixe' (see *23*, p.146); in 1921, Gaston Baty set the play in an Italianate

---

[3] F.R. Bastide, '*L'Avare* de Molière', *French Review*, 43 (1970), 654-56 (p.655).

comic tradition, making much use of mime, farce and improvisation, and in 1962, the clown-like interpretation of G. Chamarat led one critic to delight in the relief from those 'mises en scène sombres, mauriaciennes, déprimantes, qui faisaient d'Harpagon un vampire, un monstre aux doigts recourbés en pattes de crabe!'[4]

Some critics have tried to reconcile these two quite distinct views (Dullin's interpretation of the play (*4*) sought to avoid both exaggerated buffoonery and unmitigated gloom), but for many the seemingly light-hearted moments are seen merely to attenuate the grim truth of the subject. For Fernandez, the comedy's underlying cynicism is only 'allégé' by the stylisation of action and character (*25*, p.212), and Donnay concludes that, in spite of its amusing interludes, the play remains 'une pièce triste, une tragédie rosse'.[5]

Theatrical interpretations, like textual analyses, can easily be one-sided, turning the play into either a dark and demoralising tragedy or a scintillating farce. One has only to look at the various production photographs frequently included in editions of the comedy to detect different emphases. To some extent, such a wide variety of attitudes mirrors changes in critical taste. A confident grasp of the comic perspective in Molière's time gave way to greater moral consciousness in the eighteenth century and to more sombre reflectiveness in the Romantics; traces of these various trends are apparent in literary judgements of our own age. And yet *L'Avare* as a play, with its potentially disturbing subject and its lively comic mode, also reflects with particular clarity that dual function which many seventeenth-century authors ascribed to their work: *instruire* and *plaire*.

For Molière's contemporaries — writers and theatre-goers alike — comedy and tragedy were quite distinct. With its domestic settings, middle or lower class characters and plots quite devoid of political and ethical dilemmas, or serious threat of death, comedy both in the definition and the presentation of its subject could not arouse terror and pity — the response

---

[4] *Juvénal*, 2.12.1962; in M. Descotes, 'Nouvelles interprétations moliéresques', *Oeuvres et Critiques*, 6 (1981), 33-55 (p.36).

[5] M. Donnay, *Molière*, Paris: Fayard, 1911, p.294.

awakened by tragedy. Boileau's distinction between the effect of the two genres makes this point clearly:

> Le Comique, ennemi des soupirs et des pleurs,
> N'admet point en ses vers de tragiques douleurs.
>
> (*Art poétique*, Chant III)

Nevertheless, Molière was to argue that such distinctions did not thereby imply that comedy was an inferior genre, offering little more than facile entertainment. In his *Critique de l'Ecole des femmes*, Sc.6, Dorante objects strongly to the claim that 'tout l'esprit et toute la beauté sont dans les poèmes sérieux, et que les pièces comiques sont des niaiseries qui ne méritent aucune louange'; he suggests that comedy has the double aim to study man in society and to amuse the public, and that as such it demands particular skills from the dramatist. To appreciate this art in *L'Avare*, we should not simply ask if the play is sombre or funny, but rather examine how two apparently opposite purposes complement and interact with each other; how essentially serious themes may be viewed in a comic light, and how what provides amusement may also provoke deeper thought. Comedy does not trivialise its subject, but allows the audience to suspend its emotional involvement or moral judgement and to view events and characters with the clarity and balance which come with detachment. To do this the dramatist must control the angle of vision from which we see the action; it is this aspect of Molière's achievement in *L'Avare* which must be looked at first.

1. Plot and Perspective

> ... dans ce monde, il faut vivre d'adresse
> (*L'Avare*, II, 4, 778-79)

On its simplest level, the plot of *L'Avare* opposes a miser and his children in their choice of marriage partners. For Elise, Harpagon proposes the wealthy but aged Anselme; Elise herself loves Valère who has won favour as the miser's *intendant*. For Cléante, the father suggests a rich widow, who never appears on stage; he plans to take for his own wife the fair Mariane, with whom his son has also fallen in love. This opposition of youth and old age is not in itself comic. Writing towards the end of the century, La Bruyère remarked on the way excessive parental authority could have a corrosive effect on the family unit: 'Il y a d'étranges pères, et dont toute la vie ne semble occupée qu'à préparer à leurs enfants des raisons de se consoler de leur mort' ('De l'homme', 17). Nevertheless, such a conflict is often the basis of comic plots, and is presented in such a way that stress lies not so much on tense or pathetic confrontation as on the interaction of youthful enthusiasm and quick-wittedness in the lovers with rigidity, but considerable guile, in the parent. In *Le Médecin volant*, one of Molière's first farces, the heroine devises the 'bonne invention' of feigned illness as she attempts to outmanœuvre her father, whose plans for her marriage she finds quite unacceptable; and in the later *L'Ecole des femmes*, the young Horace sets out to liberate his beloved Agnès from the clutches of a jealous guardian:

> Pour moi, tous mes efforts, tous mes voeux les plus doux
> Vont à m'en rendre maître en dépit du jaloux;
>
> (I, 4, 341-42)

Comic characters of this kind do not dwell on suffering, but are given the necessary inventiveness of mind to outwit those who threaten their happiness. This same basic emphasis characterises the presentation of the young lovers in *L'Avare*.

The opening scene of the comedy is particularly important for setting this tone. As the favoured suitor of Elise, Valère has some of the qualities of a romantic hero; he has already risked his own life to rescue her from a shipwreck, and he appeals to this sensitive girl with his 'générosité surprenante' (46), 'soins pleins de tendresse' (47-48), and 'hommages assidus de cet ardent amour' (49). In the world of comedy, however, mental dexterity rather than valour defines the lover, and in order to ensure his happiness Valère does not plan to elope but endeavours instead to coax the miser into agreeing to his marriage with Elise. His present role as accomplished flatterer now eclipses past exploits as courageous hero, and at the end of the scene he expresses youthful pride at the progress he has made:

> J'y fais des progrès admirables; et j'éprouve que, pour gagner les hommes, il n'est point de meilleure voie que de se parer à leurs yeux de leurs inclinations, que de donner dans leurs maximes, encenser leurs défauts et applaudir à ce qu'ils font. (76-80)

It is not the feelings of these young lovers which will be examined in this comedy, the nature of their affection for each other, their hopes and suffering, but rather their ability to respond to the challenge to their ingenuity which the miser represents.

In I, 4, Molière puts Elise face to face with a determined Harpagon. In another of the dramatist's early plays, *Sganarelle, ou le Cocu imaginaire*, a similar confrontation takes place; the miserly Gorgibus has the brutish impatience of a tyrannical father, rapidly resorting to threats of violence to which the unfortunate Célie has only a rather whimpering 'Hélas' in reply. The rudimentary caricature of openly aggressive father and helplessly inadequate daughter becomes, in *L'Avare*, the sophisticated duel of two ideally matched opponents, a spectacle whose very stylisation ensures the necessary detachment of the audience:

> ELISE, *faisant une révérence*: Je ne veux point me marier,
> mon père, s'il vous plaît.
> HARPAGON, *contrefaisant sa révérence*: Et moi, ma petite
> fille, ma mie, je veux que vous vous mariiez, s'il vous
> plaît.
> ELISE, *faisant encore la révérence*: Je vous demande
> pardon, mon père.
> HARPAGON, *contrefaisant Elise*: Je vous demande pardon,
> ma fille. (436-441)

Stress falls not on the emotions which inspire each retort — the brutal obstinacy of a father, the frantic despair of a daughter — but rather on the form they take, on the symmetrical exchange of compliment and counter-compliment; profound disagreement is given comic expression in the very similarity of the characters' language as each ironically echoes the other. Furthermore, the effortless, mechanical repetition of such terms of deference and tractability, accompanied as they are by courteous gestures, captures the very intransigence of each speaker, father and daughter alike possessed of the same unshiftable stubbornness. Molière gives to the confrontation a smoothly balanced structure, as first Elise and then Harpagon leads the protest, only to be answered at once with a challenging riposte. Elise's defiant threats of suicide are first deflated by the miser's thrusting realism and confident authority (455-58), and then Harpagon's assertions of his own good sense are answered by his daughter's incisive appeal to reason:

> HARPAGON: C'est un parti où il n'y a rien à redire, et je
> gage que tout le monde approuvera mon choix.
> ELISE: Et moi, je gage qu'il ne saurait être approuvé
> d'aucune personne raisonnable.   (462-65)

Elise's romanticism is seen as both ineffectual and out of place, and Harpagon's claims to normality are just as rapidly undercut. Here is no tense conflict of good and evil, of frailty and tyranny, but the comic interaction of two characters who vainly seek to out-argue each other.

The dramatist's good-humoured irony at the expense of the lovers in their struggle contributes much to his successful avoidance of pathos. When, in the following scene, Valère is called upon to defend the miser's choice of a partner, his control over Harpagon, so proudly proclaimed earlier, is seen to falter when put to the test: theory and practice comically diverge. His confidence in the effectiveness of his ruse is clearly evident as he agrees spontaneously and unconditionally with the miser's opinion (476-77), but such assurance is shaken when he discovers the cause of his master's dispute. The flattery which he thought to be the ideal way of safeguarding his courtship of Elise is now seen to act against it, and the hero finds himself trapped in a role which undermines his own interests, forced to agree with the miser and yet endeavouring also to counter this threat to his love:

> Je dis que dans le fond je suis de votre sentiment, et vous ne pouvez pas que vous n'ayez raison. Mais aussi n'a-t-elle pas tort tout à fait . . .   (485-87)

Harpagon's eagerness for this particular marriage is fuelled by Anselme's willingness to marry Elise 'sans dot'. Valère tries all conceivable arguments to counter this proposal, appealing to the miser's affection for his daughter, his concern for his reputation and even to his pride as a father, but each time a stabbing repetition of 'sans dot' cuts him short. From automatic acceptance of Harpagon's reasoning ('Assurément, cela ne reçoit point de contradiction', 503), Valère is led to expressions of ever-increasing helplessness, pretended agreement coinciding exactly with a spontaneous outburst of frustration: 'Il est vrai. Cela ferme la bouche à tout: *sans dot*! Le moyen de résister à une raison comme celle-là?' (525-26). When finally he is left alone with Elise, his inadequacy is made comically plain. As the heroine laments that he has achieved little in the debate, her lover resorts again to his earlier claims to be the careful tactician, protesting once more his superior guile:

> Heurter de front ses sentiments est le moyen de tout gâter,
> et il y a de certains esprits qu'il ne faut prendre qu'en
> biaisant, des tempéraments ennemis de toute résistance,
> des naturels rétifs, que la vérité fait cabrer, qui toujours se
> raidissent contre le droit chemin de la raison, et qu'on ne
> mène qu'en tournant où l'on veut les conduire.   (534-39)

The remark reflects Valère's insight into the nature of
Harpagon's obsession, but in the comic context it suggests
equally his defeat in this encounter with the miser: controlled
flattery is much closer to helpless acceptance than the lover
would like to think. And as Elise draws his attention to the
immediate threat of her marriage to Anselme, which will hardly
leave long enough for such subtle measures to take effect, Valère
is reduced to proposing feigned illness or elopement as their
ultimate defence (551-52). In the mouth of this outmanœuvered
hero such traditional gestures of defiance are not so much the
expression of resourcefulness in the face of parental tyranny as a
tacit admission of failure. Once again, the audience's attention
in the scene is diverted from the possible suffering of the
characters; it is fixed instead on the hero's struggles to convince
Elise, and himself, that he is still in control.

On other occasions Valère's success is more striking and his
ruse given a more sophisticated comic function. In III, 1,
Harpagon endeavours to provide a supper for Mariane but is
constantly confronted by the clear and embarrassing evidence of
his parsimony: servants in worn-out livery, forced to contort
themselves in an effort to appear natural, stress the unpalatable
truth that entertainment means expense. Both in his words and
his actions the miser fails to transform meanness into normality,
falling into ridiculous utilitarianism as he instructs his servants
to serve drinks, 'mais seulement lorsque l'on aura soif' (1021).
Valère's control of language however is masterly. Whereas
Cléante in *Le Bourgeois gentilhomme* adopts the elaborate
costume of the Grand Turc to adapt to the aristocratic
pretensions of Monsieur Jourdain, Valère uses the disguise of
words, modelling himself in the image of Harpagon and

authenticating the miser's cherished vision of hospitality without expense. When Maître Jacques requests money for the meal, Valère echoes the outrage and even the terminology of the miser, rejecting this 'réponse . . . impertinente' (1083); and, turning convention on its head, he constructs a new set of social values, defending niggardliness in the name of human kindess and good sense. His horror at Maître Jacques's enthusiastic proposals for a tasty meal underlines the comic discrepancy between this new vision and the accepted one; in the house of the miser, normality has become madness and generosity is conceived as an act of aggression:

> Est-ce que vous avez envie de faire crever tout le monde? et Monsieur a-t-il invité des gens pour les assassiner à force de mangeaille? (1117-19)

Valère's performance reaches its climax as he adds to this ironical distortion a fine touch of intellectual respectability; he affirms the very sanity of the code he proposes by invoking the authority of Cicero:

> . . . c'est un coupe-gorge qu'une table remplie de trop de viandes; que, pour se bien montrer ami de ceux que l'on invite, il faut que la frugalité règne dans les repas qu'on donne; et que, suivant le dire d'un ancien, *il faut manger pour vivre, et non pas vivre pour manger*. (1123-27)

Such is his success that Harpagon, on the only occasion in the comedy, is led to speak happily of expense, proposing a particularly ostentatious and extravagant way of memorising a dictum which he finds so appealing, but which he has difficulty in repeating correctly: 'Je les veux faire graver en lettres d'or sur la cheminée de ma salle' (1137-38). Valère's skill here may indirectly reflect a further triumphant stage in his courtship of Elise as he wins the favour and confidence of the miser; significantly, though, this is not the principal focus of attention. The lover's ruse is exploited to reveal not only the intensity of the young hero's passion for Harpagon's daughter, but also the absurdity of the miser's passion for money. It is a point which will be returned to later.

The old man's love for Mariane which brings him into contact with Frosine and into conflict with his son occupies a more substantial part of the comedy, and in this plot, too, Molière draws comic effects from the efforts of characters to outwit each other. Frosine has the role of go-between who seeks to make money for herself by exploiting Harpagon's passion. La Flèche may stress the niggardliness of the miser in II, 4 ('Je te défie d'attendrir, du côté de l'argent, l'homme dont il est question', 801-02), but Frosine happily rises to this challenge to her ingenuity. Like Valère, she is proud of her divinely given talents of 'intrigue' and 'industrie' (780), and is confident of her control:

> Mon Dieu! je sais l'art de traire les hommes. J'ai le secret
> de m'ouvrir leur tendresse, de chatouiller leurs cœurs, de
> trouver les endroits par où ils sont sensibles. (798-800)

In II, 5, Molière shows the masterly schemer at work as she seizes on important traits in the miser's character — desire for longevity, scorn of the young — and reveals a mind as calculating as Harpagon's own, putting a value on all the benefits to be gained from marriage to a frugal wife; her display reaches a crescendo as she transforms negative savings into a substantial dowry:

> N'est-ce pas quelque chose de réel que de vous apporter en
> mariage une grande sobriété, l'héritage d'un grand amour
> de simplicité de parure, et l'acquisition d'un grand fonds
> de haine pour le jeu? (894-97)

Vocabulary clearly dear to the miser — 'héritage', 'acquisition', 'fonds' and the insistent repetition of 'grand' — create here an illusion of opulence, but Harpagon is not deceived. Talk of spending may for him be tantamount to spending, but talk of money is no substitute for the real thing, and from her apparently unassailable position, Frosine is forced on to the defensive. As she tries to bring the subject round to possible financial aid in a pressing law suit, she is constantly obliged to retreat and resume her flattery:

> En vérité, Monsieur, ce procès m'est d'une conséquence tout à fait grande. (*Il reprend son visage sévère.*) Je suis ruinée si je le perds, et quelque petite assistance me rétablirait mes affaires. Je voudrais que vous eussiez vu le ravissement où elle était à m'entendre parler de vous. (*Il reprend un air gai.*) (981-85)

From imminent success, Frosine is led slowly but inexorably to the brink of defeat; the character who had begun by dominating the conversation and her prey with consummate control of words finds herself dominated by the miser's unanswerable facial expressions. A scene which opened with apparent agreement between the two characters finally fragments into two quite distinct monologues — Frosine, obsessed by her own request for money now speaks of nothing else, and Harpagon, quite impervious to these pleas, offers her a form of comfort quite different from the one she requests:

> FROSINE: Je vous assure, Monsieur, que vous ne sauriez jamais me soulager dans un plus grand besoin.
> HARPAGON: Je mettrai ordre que mon carrosse soit tout prêt pour vous mener à la foire.
> FROSINE: Je ne vous importunerais pas si je ne m'y voyais forcée par la nécessité.
> HARPAGON: Et j'aurai soin qu'on soupe de bonne heure pour ne vous point faire malades. (994-1001)

Once again the dramatist's angle of vision is significant. The troubling plight of Mariane in this proposed marriage does not occupy the audience's attention: instead stress falls clearly on the skilful jousting of two minds, the thrust and parry as each character seeks to further his or her own ends.

It is the confrontation of Cléante and his father, however, which has been seen as the most problematical and disturbing element of the comedy (cf. *29*, p.96). Cléante is something of an aspiring romantic hero who would like to see himself as a provident lover, but whose dreams are constantly thwarted by uncompromising reality — the avarice of his father:

> Figurez-vous, ma sœur, quelle joie ce peut être que de relever la fortune d'une personne que l'on aime; [...] et concevez quel déplaisir ce m'est de voir que, par l'avarice d'un père, je sois dans l'impuissance de goûter cette joie et de faire éclater à cette belle aucun témoignage de mon amour. (153-60)

In 'Du cœur', 20, La Bruyère comments on the pity inspired by relationships where absence of wealth prevents the happy fulfilment of love: 'Il est triste d'aimer sans une grande fortune, et qui nous donne les moyens de combler ce que l'on aime, et le rendre si heureux qu'il n'ait plus de souhaits à faire', but Molière's focus lies rather on the comic impetuosity of the youth who lives in a dream world. His desire to give financial assistance to his beloved is inspired as much by the pleasure it will give him as by the help it will afford Mariane; without such grand romantic gestures he is unable to express himself.

In his efforts to outwit the miser, success comes no more easily to him than it does to Valère or Frosine. His first attempt puts him in the clutches of a mysterious usurer, and in his search for money he is forced to endure the most ridiculous conditions, accepting both an exorbitant rate of interest and part payment with valueless odds and ends. It is a scene which will be analysed in detail later (see Chapter 3). In Act III he resorts to other means, using ruse rather than flight to outmanœuvre his father. When Harpagon plans to welcome Mariane to his home and insists on obedience from his son, Cléante deceives the miser with studied ambiguity:

> A vous dire le vrai, mon père, je ne puis pas vous promettre d'être bien aise qu'elle devienne ma belle-mère. Je mentirais si je vous le disais. Mais pour ce qui est de la bien recevoir et de lui faire bon visage, je vous promets de

vous obéir ponctuellement sur ce chapitre. (1056-60)

Words which suggest the frankness of a son unable to conceal his true feelings yet dutifully controlling them, reflect also, for him and for the audience, a challenge to his father and an open admission of his determination to defend his love.

His meeting with Mariane in III, 7 is the sophisticated treatment of a traditional comic scene, as youth sets out to outwit old age. Bad feeling, tension and suffering are not sensed here, and attention is fixed on the linguistic skill of the lovers as they dupe their adversary. Like Valère, Cléante achieves his most significant success when he adopts attitudes which Harpagon understands and his feigned displeasure at a young stepmother-to-be who will inevitably diminish his own inheritance arouses no suspicion in a miser who can well understand such feelings:

> . . . c'est un mariage, Madame, où vous vous imaginez bien
> que je dois avoir de la répugnance; [. . .] vous n'ignorez
> pas, sachant ce que je suis, comme il choque mes intérêts.
>   (1350-52)

Content with that interpretation, Harpagon does not perceive the secondary meaning of his son's words which blend the mistrust of the stepson with the ardent declaration of the lover. The comic force of this ignorance is carefully underlined as he makes an apology to Mariane, mistaking his son's linguistic subtlety for simple bad manners: 'C'est un jeune sot qui ne sait pas encore la conséquence des paroles qu'il dit' (1367-68). Mariane, for her part, continues the deception, combining in her speech the maturity of the stepmother who likes to know where she stands, with the eagerness of the heroine delighted at this declaration of love:

> Je vous promets que ce qu'il m'a dit ne m'a point du tout
> offensée; au contraire, il m'a fait plaisir de m'expliquer
> ainsi ses véritables sentiments. J'aime de lui un aveu de la
> sorte; et, s'il avait parlé d'autre façon, je l'en estimerais

bien moins. (1369-72)

Molière then adds further variations to Cléante's demonstration of control, as the young hero openly expresses his feelings for Mariane, 'à la place de mon père' (1383), forces Harpagon into providing an elaborate and exotic supper and finally parts him from a valuable diamond ring. His revenge is presented as the comically symmetrical response to the miser's tyranny: one form of exaggerated behaviour is replaced by another. The son imposes principles of extravagance on his father just as formerly the latter had forced him into frugality; the helpless frustration which had before characterised Cléante now dominates Harpagon.

This comic interaction of two extremes is given its most sophisticated expression in the argument of father and son in IV, 2 ff. Deliberate deceit could in certain contexts be disturbing, even tragic — its potential was seized on, for instance, by Racine in *Mithridate* (III, 5), and by Corneille in *Attila* (IV, 4). Here, however, the focus is quite different. Molière does not present the manipulation of an innocent victim by a ruthless schemer, but an elaborate piece of play-acting on both sides. As the two characters set out to outwit each other, they adopt attitudes which, by appearing most normal, seem most likely to succeed: the impetuous lover chooses that of the obedient son, the miser that of the understanding father. When Harpagon suggests that Cléante himself might wish to marry Mariane, Cléante assumes an air of honest respectfulness, expressing disappointment with his father's choice and yet a readiness to obey him; the miser, for his part, expresses that common-sense from which, elsewhere, he seems to deviate so much. Nevertheless, beneath their respective protestations of filial respect and parental generosity the real feelings of each speaker are made quite plain:

CLÉANTE: Écoutez, il est vrai qu'elle n'est pas fort à mon goût; mais pour vous faire plaisir, mon père, je me résoudrai à l'épouser, si vous voulez.
HARPAGON: Moi? je suis plus raisonnable que tu ne penses.

Je ne veux point forcer ton inclination. (1609-13)

Indeed, such is the comic discrepancy between language and intention that the two characters are seen to adopt the role traditionally played by the other — it is the father, not the son, who insists that affection is a pre-requisite for marriage, and it is Cléante, not Harpagon, who argues that it is his duty simply to obey. The final emergence of the miser's true motives results in each returning to his natural role as Harpagon now insists on his authority and the son on the supremacy of love; from expressions of enlightenment the characters revert to rigid assertions:

> HARPAGON: Ne suis-je pas ton père? et ne me dois-tu pas respect?
> CLÉANTE: Ce ne sont point ici des choses où les enfants soient obligés de déférer aux pères, et l'amour ne connaît personne. (1664-66)

This see-sawing of roles continues in the next scene. The extreme views of each antagonist are transformed once more into attitudes of unselfish conciliation, not now because of their own scheming, but as a result of their inept arbitrator; from being the victims of each other, Cléante and Harpagon become the victims and fools of Maître Jacques. As they are persuaded in turn that they have been successful in their defiant opposition, they are seen to express new understanding of their rival, Harpagon promising to grant his son 'la liberté de choisir celle qu'il voudra' (1720), and Cléante to be 'le plus soumis de tous les hommes' (1729-30). This new reversal of roles carries its particular comic irony: the characters' explicit rejection of their earlier tyranny or disobedience implies their acknowledgement of its excess. Furthermore, the very ardour of such protestations underlines the force of the fixation on which it is based; words of forgiveness and enlightenment are inspired by, and depend on, the assumption that their respective obsessions have been satisfied. Their harmonious reunion which follows Maître Jacques's efforts at mediation parodies in this way a familiar comic scene of reconciliation. Beneath the exaggerated protestations of generosity, the audience is aware of the characters' mistaken belief that each has defeated the other:

CLÉANTE: Quoi! ne garder aucun ressentiment de toutes mes extravagances?

HARPAGON: C'est une chose où tu m'obliges par la soumission et le respect où tu te ranges.

CLÉANTE: Je vous promets, mon père, que jusques au tombeau je conserverai dans mon cœur le souvenir de vos bontés.

HARPAGON: Et moi, je te promets qu'il n'y aura aucune chose que tu n'obtiennes de moi. (1756-63)

The fact that they can each believe for a moment that their adversary may adapt to their own point of view underlines the absurd gullibility to which obsession may lead. But as the truth finally begins to emerge, Molière is careful to maintain the comic force of the encounter. Instead of writing an exchange of angry protestation, the dramatist suggests the irritation of each as they are forced into uncharacteristic poses: Harpagon uses the verb *donner* and Cléante turns down a gift:

HARPAGON: Et je donne ma malédiction.
CLÉANTE: Je n'ai que faire de vos dons. (1792-93)

Couched in these terms, the curse and the unrepentantly aggressive retort become the final expression of the characters' frustration in defeat, a last reminder of those roles which have availed them nothing: the generous father and the undemanding son.

Tension in the relationship of children and wealthy parents in seventeenth-century society was to be observed by La Bruyère: 'Les enfants peut-être seraient plus chers à leurs pères, et réciproquement les pères à leurs enfants, sans le titre d'héritiers . . .' ('Des biens de fortune', 67). In his presentation of this relationship, however, Molière does not suggest a disturbing confrontation but offers instead a more subtle insight into both father and son, each with his own form of comic fixation. Indeed such is the angle of vision in the comedy as a whole that we do not see individuals locked in a tense or pathetic struggle but stylised figures in a sophisticated ballet of ruses conceived and thwarted. The audience is detached, allowed to enjoy the plots and counter-plots, the ingenuity and linguistic control as each side tries to outmanœuvre the other. However, within this ballet, the nature of the miser himself emerges as a principal source of interest, the centre and to a large extent the inspiration of the action. The elaborate intrigues are not simply exploited as a form of comic entertainment in their own right, but serve as the vehicle for the probing examination of an obsession.

2. The Comedy of Obsession

Sans mentir, l'avarice est une étrange
rage (Boileau, Satire IV)

The miser is a character frequently found in the literature of
Molière's time; for poets and moralists of the seventeenth
century, such a type exerts a particular fascination. Some adopt
a morally critical attitude to avarice: La Bruyère, for instance,
vividly evokes the spiritual degeneration which the thirst for
money may bring about:

> Il y a des âmes sales, pétries de boue et d'ordure, éprises du
> gain et de l'intérêt . . . ; capables d'une seule volupté, qui
> est celle d'acquérir ou de ne point perdre; curieuses et
> avides du denier dix . . . De telles gens ne sont ni parents, ni
> amis, ni citoyens, ni chrétiens, ni peut-être des hommes: ils
> ont de l'argent ('Des biens de fortune', 58)

Tallemant des Réaux satirises the life of frugality led by Jean
Tardieu, a wealthy but infamously miserly lawyer of the time,
and stresses the corruption of one whose desire to live at the
expense of others leads both to criminal practice and shameless
scrounging:

> Pour lui il dîne toujours au cabaret, aux dépens de ceux
> qui ont affaire de lui, et le soir il ne prend que deux œufs.
> Il n'y a guère de gens à Paris plus riches qu'eux. Il a merité
> d'être pendu deux ou trois mille fois: il n'y a pas un plus
> grand voleur au monde. (*12*, I, p.658)

Others are sensitive to the potential loneliness and misery of
such a figure. Boileau, inspired also by Tardieu and his even
more parsimonious wife, reflects on the life of the wealthy pair
whose clothes are threadbare, whose house is cold and sparsely

furnished, and who have lost all desire for social conformity: in the end they are murdered by thieves and this brutal downfall is seen by the poet as both a punishment and a blessed release:

> Vingt ans j'ai vu ce Couple, uni d'un même vice,
> A tous mes Habitants montrer que l'avarice
> Peut faire dans les biens trouver la pauvreté,
> Et nous réduire à pis que la mendicité.
> Des voleurs qui chez eux pleins d'espérance entrèrent,
> De cette triste vie enfin les délivrèrent.
> Digne et funeste fruit du nœud le plus affreux
> Dont l'Hymen ait jamais uni deux Malheureux. (Satire X)

And La Bruyère, elsewhere in his *Caractères*, presents the miser as a misguided figure, the victim of suffering which is ultimately self-imposed:

> Il y a des gens qui sont mal logés, mal couchés, mal habillés et plus mal nourris; . . . qui se privent eux-mêmes de la société des hommes, et passent leurs jours dans la solitude; qui souffrent du présent, du passé et de l'avenir; . . . ce sont les avares. ('De l'homme', 114)

Other writers again take a stance of more ironical detachment, commenting on the curious discrepancy between potential comfort and actual hardship evident in the miser's life-style. The type occurs several times in the fables of La Fontaine, where the poet wrily observes the emptiness of a life in which possessions have become the end not the means, and where the individual derives no benefit from what he accumulates:

> L'avare rarement finit ses jours sans pleurs:
> Il a le moins de part au trésor qu'il enserre,
> Thésaurisant pour les voleurs,
> Pour ses parents, ou pour la terre.
>   ('Le Trésor et les deux hommes')

If not put to use, wealth is seen at best as valueless and at worst as debilitating:

> Le bien n'est bien qu'en tant que l'on s'en peut défaire.
> Sans cela c'est un mal. Veux-tu le réserver
> Pour un âge et des temps qui n'en ont plus que faire?
> La peine d'acquérir, le soin de conserver,
> Otent le prix à l'or, qu'on croit si nécessaire.
>
> ('L'Enfouisseur et son compère')

The absurd paradox that money may breed only suspicion and self-denial in those who possess it catches the acute eye of Boileau:

> Un Avare idolâtre, et fou de son argent,
> Rencontrant la disette au sein de l'abondance,
> Appelle sa folie une rare prudence,
> Et met toute sa gloire et son souverain bien,
> A grossir un trésor qui ne lui sert de rien. (Satire IV)

Finally, the type may be a comic figure of fun when a writer concentrates not on the moral degeneration, possible suffering, intellectual absurdity or social non-conformity of the attitude, but on the bizarre inventiveness of the miser's mind which can uncover a seemingly limitless range of areas where savings may be made. This focus is apparent already in Plautus's *Aulularia* where Euclio is said to keep everything, even his nail clippings, and it is typified in Scarron's *Roman comique* where Le Destin's father holds his breath when being measured for a suit so that less material will be needed and, to save food, joins his baby son at the breast of his wife. Such a figure features prominently in farce and in both Roman and French comedy, miserliness very often being one of the attributes of the father or guardian of the young heroine and thus an additional challenge to the hopeful lover — Molière's own *L'Etourdi*, *Le Médecin malgré lui* and *Les Fourberies de Scapin* contain such a character. Avarice then is clearly not in itself either tragic or comic — once again everything depends on the point of view. Against this background the nature and force of Molière's major study of the type may be more clearly analysed.

The criticism is often made that the portrayal of Harpagon is incoherent, bringing together in an unconvincing way such disparate characteristics as parsimony and bourgeois respectability, usury and love. Faguet speaks of 'mille traits d'avarice . . . ramassés sur lui qui ne concordent pas tous très bien ensemble'.[6] Other critics discuss the extent to which he is comic in a way which reflects the range of interpretations of the play as a whole considered in the Introduction. Gutwirth is uncompromising in his assessment of Harpagon as 'harsh, suspicious, unfeeling, unbefriended, loveless, inhuman, inexorable, destructive . . .' (43, p.364), a point of view widely voiced (cf. 3, p.xlvi; 22, p.189 and 35, p.253); others argue that he is naïve and harmless, an essentially ridiculous type, having, as Knutson puts it, much of the braggart soldier about him, 'full of ranting and bombast but weak and ineffectual' (29, p.98; cf. also 31, p.95).

It has been seen already that in his presentation of the miser's various scenes with his son and daughter Molière does not dwell on the misery which might be inflicted by a tyrannical father; indeed his comic angle of vision often suggests not conscious cruelty on the part of Harpagon but the unthinking, automatic responses of a machine. He has the mind of a calculator, able to compute at lightning speed the income from different sources invested at modestly usurious rates of interest (I, 4, 362-65); swift and unanswerable changes of facial expression register like a barometer the extremes of delight and displeasure which the talk of acquiring or spending money inspires in him (II, 5); and his relentless repetition of 'sans dot' (I, 5) provides an impenetrable linguistic barrier, erected to close off every threat to his money. Such exhibitions as these reflect that kind of mechanical quality which La Flèche expresses so pertinently in II, 4:

Le seigneur Harpagon est de tous les humains l'humain
le moins humain, le mortel de tous les mortels le plur dur

---

[6] E. Faguet, *En lisant Molière: l'homme et son temps, l'écrivain et son œuvre*, Paris: Hachette 1914, p.214; cf. also Sarcey, *19*, II, p.129.

et le plus serré . . . (789-91)

and which Bergson, in his essay on laughter, will identify as an essential characteristic of the comic.[7]

The absurdity implicit in miserliness is thrown into relief by a structure which on one level opposes Harpagon and normality. In spite of contemporary fashion, he persists in wearing outmoded clothes; when he plans to entertain he proposes to his chef not the most tasty food, but 'ces choses dont on ne mange guère, et qui rassasient d'abord' (1143-44); and his avarice, according to La Flèche, in II, 4, penetrates the very vocabulary he uses, distorting normal figures of speech as he banishes from his mouth all talk of spending:

> Il n'est rien de plus sec et de plus aride que ses bonnes grâces et ses caresses, et *donner* est un mot pour qui il a tant d'aversion qu'il ne dit jamais: *Je vous donne*, mais: *Je vous prête le bonjour*. (794-97)

By placing him in a domestic context, Molière creates constant pressure for the avaricious hero; if Harpagon, to some extent, threatens those around him, they also threaten him. What greater inconvenience for a miser, indeed, than to have a daughter to be married, a spendthrift son and a home to run? When others seek to draw conventional responses from him — concern for Elise, tolerance with Cléante, generosity in hospitality — he defends himself with the inexorability of a programmed machine. However, Molière explores this abnormality further, and suggests within the miser himself certain tensions which extend and refine the essential comic discrepancy.

The presentation of Harpagon's passion for Mariane is a clear example of this. It is traditional in comedy for love to overcome all other emotions. In Molière's own *L'Ecole des femmes*, III, 4, the young Horace tells of its force, so powerful that 'd'un avare à l'instant il fait un libéral' (906), and in Chappuzeau's *La Dame*

---

[7] H. Bergson, *Le Rire: essai sur la signification du comique*, Paris: P.U.F., 1975 (first published 1900).

d'intrigue, Crispin, the elderly miser, does not hesitate to lay on a splendid meal to regale his beloved Ruffine; as the servant Lisette wrily remarks in II, 9: 'Dès qu'on est amoureux, on cesse d'être avare' (*7*, p.391). In Harpagon, however, Molière presents no such simple transformation but examines instead the complexity of a passion which both reflects and conflicts with his avarice.

This aspect of the miser has been thought to reveal his particularly loathsome nature (cf. *35*, p.331), and it may seem to complement La Bruyère's remark that an old man in love is 'une grande difformité dans la nature' ('De l'homme', 111). It is clear, however, that in the context of comedy the marriage of old and young is in itself neither absurd nor horrifying: Anselme himself admits to such a project in V, 5 (2209-14) without arousing the scorn of the dramatist. Indeed, at the end of Molière's earlier *L'Ecole des maris*, the young Lisette actually wishes to marry the elderly but enlightened Ariste for whom she feels both affection and respect. Furthermore, Harpagon does not speak of coercing Mariane, but believes that the young girl loves him as he is; his planned marriage does not so much suggest deep-rooted cruelty, but comic gullibility. To this extent he stands in a tradition of amorous old men whose clumsy attempts to behave as young lovers are the focus of attention rather than any thought of suffering on the part of the intended partner. The astonishment of La Flèche in II,1 when he hears of the miser's plans ('. . . l'amour a-t-il été fait pour des gens bâtis comme lui?', 596-97), echoes an attitude familiar in farce of the time and captured in the refrain of one of Gaultier-Garguille's popular *Chansons*.[8]

> Mais de parler d'amourettes
> A qui passe soixante ans,
> C'est présenter des noisettes
> A ceux qui n'ont plus de dents.

When Harpagon eventually pays court to Mariane in III, 5,

[8] *Chansons de Gaultier-Garguille*, ed. E. Fournier, Paris: P. Jannet, 1858, ch. XVII, p.37.

his absurd awkwardness is made quite plain. Like M. Jourdain in *Le Bourgeois gentilhomme*, full of the precious pomposity he believes to be aristocratic, or Thomas Diafoirus in *Le Malade imaginaire* using the rigid rhetoric of the pedant, Harpagon vainly endeavours to impress. Persuaded by Frosine that Mariane loves old men who wear glasses, the miser readily obliges, but he clearly struggles when he tries to turn them into the pretext for a quasi-scientific demonstration of the lady's beauty and his love:

> . . . enfin c'est avec des lunettes qu'on observe les astres, et je maintiens et garantis que vous êtes un astre, mais un astre, le plus bel astre qui soit dans le pays des astres.
> (1306-09)

This attraction to a young girl is clearly presented as incongruous rather than menacing, but it is more than just a farcical interlude inserted rather arbitrarily into the plot and inconsistent with the miser's nature. It is not uncommon in comedy for old men to be as lecherous as they are wealthy. In Molière's *Le Mariage forcé*, Sc.2, Sganarelle looks forward with relish to the physical pleasure which marriage will bring ('Vous allez être à moi depuis la tête jusqu'aux pieds, et je serai maître de tout . . .'), and it is clear from the text that Harpagon has been captivated by aspects of Mariane's general bearing, 'son maintien honnête et sa douceur' (416), even though he is conscious of her poverty. When he first discusses with Frosine the progress of his courtship in II, 5, his concern about the dowry is immediately apparent, but physical and financial considerations remain closely interlinked. Ever vigilant, he is not deceived by the go-between's arguments that savings are tantamount to income; he needs far less hypothetical advantages from the arrangement, and concludes with the requirement: 'il faut bien que je touche quelque chose' (900-01). The miser's longing for tangible financial benefits echoes the desire for physical possession expressed by many an amorous old man and in her highly allusive reply, Frosine takes up the parallel, promising him the prospect of 'un certain pays où elles ont du bien dont vous serez le maître' (903). In his enthusiasm at this idea, Harpagon is led to express a wish not untypical of Sganarelle: 'Il faudra voir cela' (904). In this play on words, engineered by Frosine, the double force of Harpagon's longing is suggested: the old man's desire for union with a beautiful wife combines here with the miser's need for money and the comfort it brings. It is significant that it should be at this point that he is led to express the fear that he may lose Mariane to a younger man and consequently suffer 'certains petits désordres qui ne m'accommoderaient pas' (908-09). Harpagon's constant worry that he may lose his money inspires him now in this new unease: with women as with wealth, the prospect of happiness is constantly accompanied by concern for his security and self-respect.

This coexistence of eagerness and fear, characteristic of the miser, typifies Harpagon's attitude to himself as a lover, and distinguishes him from the traditional farcical old man who has total confidence in his continued virility. In Molière's *Le Mariage forcé*, Sc.1, Sganarelle is perfectly at his ease, defying any young man to appear 'plus frais et plus vigoureux', and in Chappuzeau's *La Dame d'intrigue*, I, 3, the elderly Géronte is quite certain of his undiminished prowess as a lover: 'L'écorce paraît vieille et le dedans est vert' (7, p.370). There are moments, certainly, when Harpagon distinguishes himself from what he sees as the superficial, even effeminate charms of the young, 'avec leur ton de poule laitée et leurs trois petits brins de barbe relevés en barbe de chat' (947-49), and scorns Cléante for belonging to a generation of 'damoiseaux flouets' (427) when he swoons in I, 4. Beneath this, however, is sensed the miser's deep-rooted insecurity. For all Frosine's claims that he is now entering the prime of life, Harpagon is quite conscious that his health is slowly declining: 'Il n'y a que ma fluxion qui me prend de temps en temps' (959-60), and he has no illusions that the passage of time may have left him unscathed: 'vingt années de moins pourtant ne me feraient point de mal, que je crois' (823-24).

The interacting desires for physical fulfilment and financial security ultimately lie at the heart of Harpagon's credulity. He is easily persuaded that Mariane, possessed of 'une aversion épouvantable pour tous les jeunes gens' (911-12), is in love with him; this readiness to believe, however, reflects not simply his own naïvety as a foolish lover but equally his very nature as a miser. The attitude which Frosine outlines appears quite natural to one who can readily understand why a young girl may wish such a marriage with a wealthy old man. Calculating self-interest and gullibility converge suggestively as Harpagon momentarily puts himself in Mariane's place: 'En effet, si j'avais été femme, je n'aurais point aimé les jeunes hommes' (936-37), a truth seized on at once by Frosine: 'Je le crois bien' (938). It is significant, then, that when Mariane meets Harpagon and his family in III, 6, the miser should show embarrassment that he has 'de si grands enfants' (1334-35). His unease, though, is inspired less by this evident contradiction of his status as a young lover than by his awareness that children of a first marriage are unpopular with second wives: one of the advantages of Anselme as a partner for Elise was indeed the fact that no children survived from his first marriage (I, 5, 490-91). In his defence, the miser does not reiterate protestations of youthfulness, but rather assures his intended that he will soon be rid of these burdens. Harpagon's instinctive but unconscious understanding of why the young may favour the old becomes here a vital factor in his vulnerability to deception: avarice is seen to carry the seeds of its own undoing.

Unlike Euclio in Plautus's *Aulularia*, Molière's miser is not a poor man who suddenly finds wealth, but a rich bourgeois who wishes to acquire still more; frugality is not born from his being accustomed to poverty, but from a more profound attachment to money. This is immediately apparent in Harpagon's obsessive desire not to appear rich. He accuses La Flèche in I, 3 of encouraging rumours about his wealth and in I, 4 he reproaches his children even more explicitly:

De pareils discours et les dépenses que vous faites seront cause qu'un de ces jours on me viendra chez moi couper la gorge, dans la pensée que je suis tout cousu de pistoles.
(338-40)

Even to speak of his having money is to expose him to the threat
of attack. For a contemporary audience, this fear for his life
might have recalled the downfall of Tardieu and his wife, killed
by thieves (on August 24 1665) just three years before the first
performance of Molière's play, but it suggests also the miser's
almost physical identification with his money. In II, 4, La Flèche
remarks astutely that to speak to him of expense is tantamount
to an attack on his life ('C'est le frapper par son endroit mortel,
c'est lui percer le cœur, c'est lui arracher les entrailles', 806-07),
and when in III, 1 Maître Jacques mentions the subject,
Harpagon recoils as if threatened by assault (1079-82).
Significantly, when he expresses the wish that Mariane's mother
provide a dowry for her daughter, he speaks of it in terms of
blood-letting ('Lui as-tu dit qu'il fallait . . . qu'elle se saignât
pour une occasion comme celle-ci?', 867-69), and in the
monologue which follows the discovery that he has been robbed,
images of loss and of death are constantly interlinked and lead
to the very disintegration of his sanity. The risk of theft may
indeed imply the risk of being murdered, but for Harpagon the
two fates are ultimately inseparable: wealth is his very being; to
lose it is to lose his identity.

It is this profound dependence on his money which inspires
Harpagon's attempt to exclude from his household all dissent
from his views, and to surround himself only with those who do
not threaten him; attitudes, even words, only meet with
approval when they authenticate his vision. When Valère praises
the ethic of *sans dot* he is delighted ('voilà parlé comme un
oracle', 581); when Maître Jacques tells him of outside opinion
he is not ('Apprenez à parler', 1223). The result, though, is a
fragile illusion, and the miser has to make a conscious and
constant effort to keep it intact. His first words in the comedy
are significantly those of rejection and a call for silence as he
dismisses one who challenges and questions him ('Hors d'ici tout
à l'heure, et qu'on ne réplique pas!', 184), and for all his
protestations of confidence, his underlying unease is clearly
suggested. Following his argument with Elise in I, 5, he proudly
claims that his choice is quite reasonable ('je gage que tout le
monde approuvera mon choix', 462-63), and yet it is to the

sycophantic Valère that he turns for approval; and when in the argument with his son in IV, 4 he calls to Maître Jacques for support, his request significantly carries the slight hint of a threat: 'Je te veux faire toi-même, maître Jacques, juge de cette affaire, pour montrer comme j'ai raison' (1684-85).

Harpagon's illusion ultimately cannot protect him either from others or from himself, and like the comic lover who makes himself more vulnerable the more he seeks to conceal the object of his desires, Harpagon brings himself trouble the more he attempts to keep his money. His frequent visits to the garden draw attention to the treasure he has buried there; his parsimony of II, 5 finally loses him the services of Frosine, and turns her to Mariane; and his very project of re-marriage brings with it, inevitably, the necessity of expense. Such indeed is the nature of his obsession that he is unable to keep quiet about his wealth. In I, 3 he accuses La Flèche of spreading rumours about him, but by so doing brings into the open himself the talk of money he seeks to stifle in others: 'Ne serais-tu point homme à aller faire courir le bruit que j'ai chez moi de l'argent caché?' (209-11). This same obsessive mistrust is his undoing in I, 4 when he thinks that his children have overheard his expression of delight at the newly acquired treasure he has buried in the garden. Quite unable to believe himself safe, even though it is clear to the audience that his monologue has not been overheard, Harpagon falls further and further into self-disclosure, giving more away the more he endeavours to cover his tracks (308-11): compulsive suspicion translates every gesture from Elise and Cléante as a threat, and yet his greatest enemy is himself. His expression of despair at the start of the scene: 'O Ciel! je me serai trahi moi-même' (294) carries its own suggestive truth and the miser is seen to sense it. As he tries to convince his children that he is poor, he remarks clear-sightedly on the attitude of misery which has become his own:

> Plût à Dieu que je les eusse, dix mille écus! . . . Cela m'accommoderait fort . . . Et je ne me plaindrais pas, comme je fais, que le temps est misérable. (318, 324, 326-27)

In this pretence before his family, he is evidently conscious that
wealth is normally seen as the guarantee of contentment; and
yet, knowing as he does that in spite of his riches he has found
no comfort, he is clearly aware also of the impasse in which he is
caught. Seeking permanence and fulfilment in money, he finds
himself the prey instead to suspicion, jealousy and fear; the
miser's form of self-definition is at the same time his torment. It
is against this background that the full comic significance of II,2
may be appreciated, where Harpagon, inadvertently, is seen to
turn against himself. The extent of his mistrust is ironically
reflected in his enquiry into the wealth of the family of his young
debtor-to-be, unaware that this is his own son, and the self-
defeating force of his suspicion suggestively implied as he
welcomes with the curt remark: 'C'est quelque chose que cela'
(725) the promise of what is, unbeknown to him, his own death.

For all his apparent dismissal of traditional values, the miser
is unable to live at ease in his own cocoon and his very household
reflects the ambiguity of an obsession which both defies and
fears the outside world: he has servants, however ill-clad,
horses, however badly fed, both cook and groom, albeit in the
same person. Such behaviour may seem to imply a vanity quite
out of place in a miser; in Harpagon, though, sensitivity to the
opinion of others suggests not so much a contradiction of
avarice, but an extension of the desire for self-protection which
lies at its heart. This wariness is evident, for instance, in the
conditions he lays down as the anonymous money-lender of
II, 1. By introducing a third party into the arrangement, a
usurious miser of whom he claims also to be the victim,
Harpagon clearly hopes to acquire an extra defence against
discovery and to present to the observer an image of
respectability:

> . . . pour faire plaisir à l'emprunteur il est contraint lui-
> même de l'emprunter d'un autre sur le pied du denier
> cinq . . . (640-42)

The resultant rates of interest are monstrous, the *denier cinq*
being double the rate charged by even La Bruyère's 'âmes sales',

but the discrepancy between word and intention does not simply reflect cruelty or hypocrisy in the character. Behind the façade of generosity which he clumsily seeks to present to Maître Simon is suggested self-conscious uncertainty as he pursues the usurious bargain and yet fears to state the case openly: 'La charité, Maître Simon, nous oblige à faire plaisir aux personnes lorsque nous le pouvons' (725-26). The miser's awkwardness as he tries to protect himself from the gaze of others recalls and is reflected in his instructions to La Merluche, who must contort himself in order to hide his tattered livery: 'Rangez cela adroitement du côté de la muraille, et présentez toujours le devant au monde' (1035-36).

Harpagon is indeed clearly concerned about his reputation. In I, 3 he turns on La Flèche who, in his frustration, curses misers — this scene will be discussed in Chapter 4 — and in III, 1 he urges Maître Jacques to tell him how he is regarded in the world at large. More than the simple pretext for a comic portrait of the miser, such as is given by Pythodicus in the *Aulularia* II, 4, this demand reflects the hero's obsession with others' opinion of him. Not only is Harpagon present to hear the account — unlike Euclio in Plautus's comedy — but he actually solicits it, moving from a simple nonchalant question ('Pourrais-je savoir de vous, maître Jacques, ce que l'on dit de moi?', 1189-90) to the more insistent plea: 'C'est me faire plaisir, et je suis bien aise d'apprendre comme on parle de moi' (1196-97). The suggestions of fear and shame implied in the enquiry are echoed in Maître Jacques's crowning example of his master's parsimony:

Celui-ci [conte] que l'on vous surprit une nuit en venant dérober vous-même l'avoine de vos chevaux; et que votre cocher, qui était celui d'avant moi, vous donna dans l'obscurité je ne sais combien de coups de bâton dont vous ne voulûtes rien dire. (1210-13)

The miser is seen here to have brought suffering on himself through his own meanness, and yet fear of mockery shames him into silence about the blows he has endured; he may dismiss the incriminating servant ('celui d'avant moi'), and yet his attempt to cover up his indignity has clearly failed; the world talks about it. The comic force of the servant's assessment lies not simply in its acute portrayal of a miser who is 'la fable et la risée de tout le monde' (1216), but in the reaction of Harpagon himself. Once more he is seen to be the cause of his own discomfiture, not just by having first requested this character sketch which so upsets him, but also, more significantly, by living a life which attracts the attention of the outside world which he so fears. With this *cocher*, as with his last one, his only recourse is to violence, the ultimate expression of his frustration.

Harpagon is comic not because in its extreme form avarice becomes laughable — Balzac's Grandet is no less parsimonious, and yet is a terrifying creation. It is rather because the attention of the audience is constantly drawn to the absurdity of the fixation, apparent not simply in the clash between normality and abnormality, but in the contradictions within the miser himself: inventiveness is balanced by incompetence, authority by gullibility. Many of the qualities which characterise Harpagon may be seen in other misers of the time, but the great originality of Molière is that he moulds them into a coherent whole, each trait revealing the central obsession; love, usury, and concern about reputation each in their different ways reflect both the search for security which underlies an insatiable desire for wealth and the vulnerability which inevitably accompanies it. The result is not an individualised 'character' but the embodiment of avarice with its paradoxical blend of confidence and suspicion, desire and frustration. From traditional material Molière creates something peculiarly his own. It is a process characteristic of the dramatist throughout the comedy and must now be discussed in more detail.

3. Imitation and Originality

Il m'est permis, disoit Molière, de re-
prendre mon bien où je le trouve . . .
(14, p.39)

Molière's tendency to find inspiration in other writers is well
known, and his close adaptations of classical texts (e.g.
Amphitryon, *L'Ecole des maris* or *Les Fourberies de Scapin*) or
more general echoes of contemporary French dramatists, Italian
comedy and farce have often been discussed.[9] Only a few
decades after the creation of *L'Avare*, Riccoboni was to suggest
that this comedy in particular had barely 'quatre scènes qui
soient inventées par Molière' (*17*, p.186), and, in more recent
times, critics have taken pains to seek sources for the principal
characters and incidents, constructing full and elaborate lists: a
rivalry of father and son is found in Donneau de Visé's *La Mère
coquette* (1666), a miser in love in Chappuzeau's *La Dame
d'intrigue* (1662), a usury incident in Boisrobert's *La Belle
Plaideuse* (1655), the scheming flattery of a go-between in
Ariosto's *I suppositi* (1509), and in Plautus's *Aulularia* a variety
of ideas, from the miser's confusion of his *cassette* and his
daughter to his obsession with a marriage *sans dot*, from his
suspicion of a servant to his anguished monologue on the theft
of his money. Such an autopsy may leave the impression that the
play is simply derivative; indeed one critic has gone as far as to
say that it is 'la moins originale des grandes œuvres de Molière'
(Fernandez, *25*, p.211).

It is, however, a hazardous task to look for 'sources' and can
lead to seriously misleading conclusions. *L'Avare* carries echoes
of a wide range of popular themes, present in many different
theatrical traditions: the characters of miser and lover, servant
and go-between, go back to classical antiquity and are
transmitted through Italian and French Renaissance comedy,

---

[9] See Attinger, *21*; W. Salzmann, *Molière und die lateinische Komödie*,
Heidelberg: Winter, 1969; P.A. Wadsworth, *Molière and the Italian Theatrical
Tradition*, York, SC: French Literature Publications Company, 1977.

farce and *commedia dell'arte*. Equally, the basic outlines of the plot which opposes young and old, resourceful and gullible, are quite conventional. It is often a matter of pure speculation where the dramatist's initial inspiration may have come from, if indeed there was a single spark of this kind. Furthermore, where more substantial parallels may be found, these do not necessarily imply a lack of imagination. After all, any work of literature reflects to a lesser or greater extent the tradition in which it is written. Originality is not synonymous with novelty, and the original artist is the one who creates something peculiarly his own from the common heritage. Much of the finest Renaissance love poetry in France is a creative re-working of classical and Italian models; La Fontaine's fables give new depth and suggestiveness to the originals of Aesop and Phaedrus; and the myths of antiquity have provided themes and characters which dramatists as different as Racine and Sartre have transformed and adapted to their own particular times and purposes.

In the case of *L'Avare*, comparison of model and adaptation often reveals not slavish imitation but, on the contrary, the richness of Molière's originality. One such incident is the confrontation of Cléante and his father in II, 1 f. In Boisrobert's *La Belle Plaideuse*, Ergaste, is, like Cléante, short of money and arranges to borrow from a usurer in order to further his courtship of the heroine. In I, 4 of this play, his servant Filipin tells him that he will have to borrow at the *denier dix*; although angered at this rate of interest, Ergaste agrees. At the end of the scene he discovers that the usurer is his father. In a second incident later in the play (IV, 2), the lover has a further attempt to borrow money and falls into the hands of one who tries to pass off worthless objects as part of the deal. In their broad outlines these events correspond to the sequence of scenes in *L'Avare*, but the dramatist completely transforms their impact. Molière does not reveal at once the full details of the usurer's proposals but instead there is the initial suggestion of a reasonable deal in which the money will be lent at only slightly above the legal rate (626-38). Against this background the effect of the final conditions is radically altered. The focus of attention becomes not the usury itself but the terms in which it is expressed: the more exorbitant the lender's demands the more emphatic his protestations of kindness; and his desire to 'ne charger sa conscience d'aucun scrupule' (635-36) grows into the claim that he acts 'pour faire plaisir à l'emprunteur' (640). The requirement of accepting bric-à-brac, part of a completely separate incident in the source, becomes in Molière's text the culmination of a gradual descent into absurdity. Boisrobert's lender had offered exotic animals ('guenons' and 'fort beaux perroquets') together with 'douze gros canons' (6, p.571); Molière's character prepares a much lengthier list of increasingly bizarre 'hardes' and 'nippes', ranging from items of massive furniture or outdated *objets d'art* to pieces whose value and utility the lender himself is scarcely able to maintain:

Plus un luth de Bologne garni de toutes ses cordes, ou peu s'en faut . . . Plus une peau d'un lézard de trois pieds et demi remplie de foin, curiosité agréable pour pendre au plancher d'une chambre. (679-80, 683-84)

This carefully developed movement serves in part to set Cléante in a comic light, as he descends from early expressions of hope to sheer disbelief at the ever more ridiculous conditions. In Boisrobert's play, the servant Filipin offers Ergaste a stern warning about being caught in such 'pièges d'enfer', remarking on the 'estranges manies' of the young who impetuously fall victim to them (6, p.555). La Flèche, however, has no such moralising role, as he raises his master's expectations and constantly increases his frustration by slowly reading out the inventory and the 'quelques petites conditions' (614). His wry reference to Panurge clearly sets Cléante in a comic tradition — such readiness to accept the miser's terms in order to satisfy his ambitious heroic plans is seen as just a small step from the extravagant mismanagement of Rabelais's hero who fritters away a vast fortune in the space of a few days:

Je vous vois, Monsieur, ne vous en déplaise, dans le grand chemin justement que tenait Panurge pour se ruiner,

prenant argent d'avance, achetant cher, vendant à bon
marché, et mangeant son blé en herbe. (696-99)

In this context, his bitter indictment of Harpagon says just as
much about himself as about the father he curses; the
imprecation of parental avarice is the only means left to express
his frustration at the apparent failure of his schemes.

But if Molière's adaptation of Boisrobert's scenes gives
greater comic force to the young hero, it also has a further
function. In *La Belle Plaideuse* the character of the lender is
little defined and the figure of the father has not at this point
appeared in the play — there is thus no hint that they are the
same person; in *L'Avare*, however, Molière gives to the usurer
traits of suspicion already familiar to the audience. La Flèche is
quite mystified by the care which the moneylender has taken to
conceal his identity (617-19) and in the opening conditions it is
clear that this shadowy figure distinguishes himself less for his
tyranny than for his supreme caution:

> Supposé que le prêteur voie toutes ses sûretés, et que
> l'emprunteur soit majeur et d'une famille où le bien soit
> ample, solide, assuré, clair et net de tout embarras, on fera
> une bonne et exacte obligation par-devant un notaire, le
> plus honnête homme qu'il se pourra et qui, pour cet effet,
> sera choisi par le prêteur, auquel il importe le plus que
> l'acte soit dûment dressé. (628-33)

As has been seen already the particular terms of the deal reflect
Harpagon's desire to preserve an image of respectability, and
this culminates in his protestations of good faith as he makes the
final valuation of his useless objects:

> Le tout, ci-dessus mentionné, valant loyalement plus de
> quatre mille cinq cents livres, et rabaissé à la valeur de
> mille écus par la discrétion du prêteur. (685-87)

In this way Molière adds a new dimension to Boisrobert's
original, creating the promise of a comic encounter between two

characters whose feelings of self-satisfaction are as precarious as
their meeting with each other is imminent; Cléante, although
frustrated, believes that he has outwitted his father, and
Harpagon, although cautious, believes that he has managed to
conceal a fine piece of business from the outside world. Both
characters, however, are deceived and the meeting which follows
will shatter their illusions.

When Amidor meets his son in Boisrobert's play, Ergaste's
discomfort is immediately apparent and his father is furious at
what he sees. With evident assurance and maturity, he proceeds
to upbraid Ergaste for his prodigality, developing a moral
argument which both justifies his own apparent parsimony as a
father and delivers an eloquent criticism of the son whose
wasteful habits make such paternal stringency necessary.

> Si tu te contentais d'un entretien honnête,
> Tu m'aurais vu bon père, et selon ton état,
> Je t'aurais fait paraître avec assez d'éclat;
> Mais tes profusions lassent ma patience,
> Il y va de l'honneur et de la conscience.
>
> 　　　　　　　　　　　　　(6, I, 8, p.558)

Ergaste is left silenced: his father may be harsh but he is not
ridiculous. Boisrobert's scene, though, is completely
transformed by Molière. No equivalent moral lesson is
delivered, and when Harpagon and Cléante meet, the dramatist
concentrates attention on the explosion of their mutual
annoyance as each goes into the attack, each by implication,
criticising his own as well as the other's excesses:

> HARPAGON: Comment! pendard, c'est toi qui t'aban-
> 　　donnes à ces coupables extrémités?
> CLÉANTE: Comment! mon père, c'est vous qui vous portez
> 　　à ces honteuses actions? (740-43)

The miser's sense of guilt spills out into reproof of his son;
Cléante's feelings of shame are reflected in this accusation of his
father. In the exchange which follows, Harpagon, embarrassed

at being caught out, rages at his son's quite incomprehensible
lack of financial sense, and Cléante, frustrated in defeat, points
to the absurd extent of his father's usury:

> HARPAGON: C'est toi qui te veux ruiner par des emprunts
>   si condamnables?
> CLÉANTE: C'est vous qui cherchez à vous enrichir par des
>   usures si criminelles?
> HARPAGON: Oses-tu bien, après cela, paraître devant moi?
> CLÉANTE: Osez-vous bien, après cela, vous présenter aux
>   yeux du monde?
>
> (744-50)

The miser's attempts to judge Cléante's actions by his own
values are tellingly countered by his son's appeal to the
judgement of the outside world which, as has been seen already,
Harpagon both rejects and fears. It is significant that his final
response to Cléante should not be to look him straight in the eye,
as Boisrobert's miser does, or to call on a third party to
arbitrate. Finding himself vulnerable to attack when he had
sought to protect himself so well, his only recourse is to dismiss
his son from his sight: 'Ôte-toi de mes yeux, coquin, ôte-toi de
mes yeux!' (760). At the end of the scene, stress lies not on the
plight of the young lover, resolved more than ever to acquire
funds, as is the case in *La Belle Plaideuse*, but on Harpagon
himself, irritated not simply by the disobedience of his son, but
by his own exposure. Arnavon speaks of this meeting as 'une
situation poignante' (*35*, p.233) and it would indeed be possible
to play the encounter in this way; but when La Flèche describes
it in the next scene as 'tout à fait drôle' (770) the intended
register is clear.

This comparison with a 'source' reveals important features of
Molière's art. His creative theatrical sense is suggested not
simply in his amplification of certain details, but in the
fundamental restructuring of diverse elements into a harmonious whole which encourages the audience both to expect
and to enjoy the meeting of father and son. Furthermore, he
lends a greater comic force to the protagonists themselves,

making of the young lover a hero as ridiculous as he is penetrating, and of the miser an old man as gullible as he is tyrannical. Boisrobert's simple opposition of sound moral sense and youthful extravagance is transformed as a consequence into a more subtle encounter in which each character is confronted not simply with his adversary, but with evidence of his own foolishness.

The second scene to be discussed in this context is perhaps the most celebrated and complex in the play: Harpagon's monologue in IV, 7. The misery which follows the loss of wealth was commented on by La Bruyère: 'Il n'y a qu'une affliction qui dure, qui est celle qui vient de la perte des biens' ('Des biens de fortune', 76), and in La Fontaine's fable 'L'Avare qui a perdu son trésor', the miser is reduced to violent anguish when he discovers that he has been robbed:

Voilà mon homme aux pleurs; il gémit, il soupire,
Il se tourmente, il se déchire . . .

The theme is traditional, but a particular source for Molière's scene is constantly remarked on: the speech of Euclio in Plautus's *Aulularia*, a speech itself imitated by Lorenzo de Medici in his *Aridosia* (1536) and by Larivey in his adaptation of this, *Les Esprits* (1579). In terms of its principal themes, Molière's scene clearly has much in common with the Roman text: the aimlessness of the miser, the suicidal despair, the appeal to the audience, the self-pity are apparent in both, but from these bare bones, Molière creates a speech which has its own particular character.

From the outset, Molière emphasises the discrepancy between the extent of the miser's despair and the cause of it. To Euclio's opening outburst of abstract lament: 'Je suis perdu, je suis assassiné, je suis mort!'[10] Molière adds specific images of theft and murder, whose stark conjunction underlines the incongruity of the event and Harpagon's reaction to it: 'Je suis perdu, je suis assassiné, on m'a coupé la gorge, on m'a dérobé mon argent'

---

[10] The translation is by the abbé de Marolles, in *Les Comédies de Plaute*, 4 vols (1658); text cited in Couton, *1*, II, p.1395.

(1808-09); this is prefaced by a cry for help which yokes similarly discordant images for the same effect: 'Au voleur! au voleur! à l'assassin! au meurtrier!' (1806-07). This juxtaposition, sustained throughout the monologue, clearly intensifies the comic force of the speech, but, more than this, it reflects the essential vulnerability of the miser for whom money and life are inextricably linked. Figurative language of mortal despair at his loss descends into the grotesque vision of his burial as the miser pretends to be dead and then appeals for news of his treasure which will be his resurrection:

> C'en est fait, je n'en puis plus; je me meurs, je suis mort, je suis enterré. N'y a-t-il personne qui veuille me ressusciter en me rendant mon cher argent, ou en m'apprenant qui l'a pris? (1818-20)

Present neither in Plautus, nor in other subsequent adaptations of the speech, this gesture has its particular significance. In other comedies of Molière characters feign death in order to outwit those who wish to outwit them — Angélique deceives Georges Dandin with such a trick in *Georges Dandin*, III, 6, just as Argan deceives Béline in *Le Malade imaginaire*, III, 12. Unlike Molière's other comic protagonists, however, Harpagon is alone on stage, and the enemy he seeks to outwit is both unknown and unseen; performed thus in a void, the familiar farcical ploy becomes the more suggestive reflection of an obsession which can isolate and debilitate its victim.

In both Plautus and Molière, the miser addresses the audience in his search for comfort and enlightenment, a breaking of theatrical illusion which is traditional in farce. In the *Aulularia*, Euclio begs for help, but as he notices the public's laughter he turns to a stinging attack on their dishonest ways:

> Ils se cachent sous des habits modestes, sous la blancheur de la craie, et se tiennent assis comme des personnes sérieuses.

In Molière, however, this gesture is used not as the pretext for social satire but to suggest more about the miser himself, whose mistrust of his household has now suddenly extended into mistrust of everyone:

> Que de gens assemblés! Je ne jette mes regards sur personne qui ne me donne des soupçons, et tout me semble mon voleur. (1826-28)

Harpagon is subjected here to a comic form of agoraphobia: he is unable to hide anywhere from his obsession. The audience is fashioned in the image of the miser's suspicion, and every little noise increases and intensifies his torment; their eventual laughter is the final crescendo in a series of mysterious and threatening sounds:

> Euh! que dites-vous? Ce n'est personne . . . Eh! de quoi est-ce qu'on parle là? de celui qui m'a dérobé? Quel bruit fait-on là-haut? Est-ce mon voleur qui y est? De grâce, si l'on sait des nouvelles de mon voleur, je supplie que l'on m'en dise. N'est-il point caché là parmi vous? Ils me regardent tous et se mettent à rire. (1820-21, 1828-32)

It is in this evocation of a self-tormenting mania that Molière differs most suggestively from Plautus. Both Euclio and Harpagon rage in helpless fury, both search vainly for the cause of their misery, piling question on question as their desperation grows, but whereas Euclio is left in an aimless search for a robber who alone is the cause of his despair, Harpagon is led again and again into conflict with himself. Euclio calls out blindly to stop a thief he can visualise for a fleeting moment: 'Tenez, tenez celui qui m'a volé. Mais qui est-il?' Harpagon grasps his own arm in a farcical gesture of self-aggression:

> N'est-il point là? N'est-il point ici? Qui est-ce? Arrête! (*Il se prend lui-même le bras.*) Rends-moi mon argent, coquin! . . . Ah! c'est moi. (1811-13)

Later, in another divergence from the source, Harpagon

contemplates an appeal to justice; longing to question everyone he can only fall into absurdity as he adds himself to the list of suspects:

> Je veux aller querir la justice et faire donner la question à toute ma maison: à servantes, à valets, à fils, à fille, et à moi aussi. (1824-26)

And at the end of the scene, when Harpagon contemplates suicide, this same emphasis is clear. Euclio may see no purpose in living, but, significantly, Harpagon's desire for death follows on at once from his proposed execution of the whole world, whom he now accuses of causing his suffering; despair converges with self-punishment:

> Je veux faire pendre tout le monde; et, si je ne retrouve mon argent, je me pendrai moi-même après. (1835-36)

Through physical gesture or linguistic illogicality Molière suggests all that is essentially self-defeating in avarice, the miser's very search for satisfaction in wealth bringing with it his own frustration.

For all the apparent emotional intensity of the speech, this monologue is comic. Harpagon demonstrates none of the qualities which characterise the tragic hero — dignity in adversity, heroic self-awareness, a positive response to the inevitability of suffering for which he assumes partial responsibility — and the farcical elements in language and action which Molière adds to his source ensure that this perspective is clear at the moment of performance. Significantly, however, such moments are not inserted simply as an end in themselves to increase the appeal of the speech as comic entertainment, but as a means of revealing different facets of the miser's obsession; by making us laugh, Molière invites us also to understand. This interaction of *divertissement* and insight which underlies the dramatist's comic art will now be examined further.

4. Stylisation and Realism

Un coup d'œil, un pas, un geste, tout y
était observé avec une exactitude qui
avait été inconnue jusque-là sur les
théâtres de Paris. (La Grange, Preface
to *Œuvres de M. de Molière* (1682);
see *1,* I, p.1001)

Molière has often been seen to offer a faithful portrait of
everyday life in his comedies. Wilson speaks of the dramatist's
aim being 'truth to life and naturalness' (*3,* p.xxxviii) and
Mornet sees in the language of each character 'le style ou
l'absence de style qu'il aurait réellement dans la vie'.[11] Applied
to the play's setting such words as 'realistic' or 'natural' have
some sense insofar as the action takes place in a recognisable
domestic milieu not far removed in either time or locality from
the world of the audience. References to contemporary reality
are also to be found in the fabric of the comedy, from moments
of historical truth — there *was* a revolt in Naples in 1647-48
(V, 5, 2164) — to glimpses of the original actors in the
dramatist's troupe — the limping Louis Béjart who played La
Flèche (I, 3, 282), the coughing Molière who played Harpagon
(II, 5, 959-60). Furthermore, Harpagon has many of the traits
one sees recorded in accounts of contemporary misers —
outdated clothes, undernourished servants and horses, aversion
to entertaining.[12] Nevertheless it is equally true that all
seemingly 'realistic' literature does not and cannot approximate
to a photographic representation of reality. In all forms of art —
even indeed photography — the artist operates choices of detail
and perspective, giving form and order to what he sees, so as to
convey his sense of what is essential in the subject. Molière, like

[11] D. Mornet, *Molière*, Connaissance des Lettres, 11, Paris: Boivin, 1943,
p.183.

[12] See for example the descriptions of Tardieu in Tallemant's *Historiettes*, or
Boileau's Satire X.

every other writer, does not offer a slice of life but a structured, artistic vision.

It is clear, indeed, that *L'Avare* is not 'realistic' in its presentation of action and character. As has already been seen in different contexts, language does not necessarily follow the natural rhythms of everyday speech but is characterised by its rich texture of echo and variation, counterpoint and contrast; Robinet, commenting in his *Lettre en vers* on the first performances, referred to this particularly:

> Il parle en prose, et non en vers;
> Mais nonobstant les goûts divers,
> Cette prose est si théâtrale
> Qu'en douceur les vers elle égale.
>   (15.9.1668; see *15*, I, p.319)

In costume, too, details are seized on, not simply to produce an authentic image of reality, but to reveal character: the worn-out livery of the servants, the uniforms of Maître Jacques, the old-fashioned garb of Harpagon, the ribbons of Cléante all in their different ways capture essential features of the miser and his household, as do indeed the very names they have, from the traditionally romantic Valère and Cléante, Elise and Mariane, to the suggestions of undernourishment in Brindavoine ('whisker' of oats) or La Merluche (dried cod), cunning in La Flèche (arrow) or grasping obstinacy in Harpagon himself (harpago (lat.): grappling iron). Indeed the play has much in common with Italian improvised comedy, that most stylised of theatrical forms, in its use of caricature, mime and physical action. The miser's constant moves outside (I, 5; II, 3; III, 8), the frequent changes of his facial expression (II, 5), the ironical, courteous gestures to his daughter (I, 4), his fall (III, 9), his violence (I, 3; III, 1; III, 3), are complemented by the servants' awkward poses (III, 1), Maître Jacques's hasty changes of costume (III, 1) or his argument with Valère (III, 2). Riccoboni would later single out scenes in this play as typical *canevas* of the *commedia dell'arte* (notably II, 5; III, 2; III, 7; IV, 4 and 5) and such is the nature of the comedy that it has lent itself to constant elaborations and additions of stage business in productions over the centuries (see *23*, p.136).

Such stylisation has been seen already as something of an antidote to the tension and pathos potential in the plot, as it presents the audience not with rounded characters in conflict but with a carefully controlled ballet; more than this, though, it is an essential part of the rich theatrical entertainment offered by the comedy. Molière himself was a particularly skilful and expressive actor, a talent testified to by his contemporaries, and most notably by Neufvillenaine who left a revealing account of his interpretation of the foolish and suspicious husband in *Le Cocu imaginaire*. The dimension of performance is lost when one reads the text of *L'Avare*, and one can only surmise the peculiar force of a scene like II, 5 where word and gesture interact across shifts from contentment to disapproval, or imagine the constant changes of expression which would doubtless have accompanied the monologue of IV, 7 as the miser ranges from acute despair to manic glee, from frantic hallucination to fragile calm. At moments like these, the words we see on the page are little more than the notes of a score, a guide only to the full power of the comedy; language indeed is just a part, the only surviving element of a totality now lost, and which Molière, writing as he was for himself, could visualise in its entirety. For Neufvillenaine, performance was as skilful as original conception, and the two could not be separated:

L'on n'a jamais vu tenir de discours si naïfs, ni paraître avec un visage si niais, et l'on ne doit pas moins admirer l'auteur pour avoir fait cette pièce, que pour la manière dont il la représente. (see, *1*, I, p.1233)

The skill with which *L'Avare* was first performed is testified to in Robinet's *Lettre en vers* (15.9.1668):

Au reste, il est si bien joué,
(C'est un fait de tous avoué)
Par toute sa troupe excellente . . .

                              (see *15*, I, p.319)

and when we read the text we should recall Molière's own injunction to the reader of his *L'Amour médecin*, reminding him that the full pleasure of the comedy can only be grasped when it is read as a 'play':

> . . . on sait bien que les comédies ne sont faites que pour être jouées, et je ne conseille de lire celle-ci qu'aux personnes qui ont des yeux pour découvrir dans la lecture tout le jeu du théâtre.

Significantly, though, such *jeux de théâtre* are not conceived simply as providing incidental entertainment but as contributing to the meaning of the play. Molière clearly understood how the rich language of gesture could be used to convey mood and character, and the early commentaries on his performance in *Le Cocu imaginaire* underline his power of expression:

> son visage et ses gestes expriment si bien la jalousie, qu'il ne serait pas nécessaire qu'il parlât pour paraître le plus jaloux de tous les hommes. (see *1*, I, p.1229)

The constant interaction of stylisation and suggestiveness implied on the level of performance is also apparent in the text itself. The meeting of Harpagon and La Flèche in I, 3, for example, is a scene, adapted from Plautus, which has been considered slight and *invraisemblable* by critics at various times. Fénelon was unimpressed by Harpagon's desire to see the servant's 'other hands', arguing that only a madman would act in this way:

> . . . un avare qui n'est point fou ne va jamais jusqu'à vouloir regarder dans la troisième main de l'homme qu'il soupçonne de l'avoir volé . . . (*13*, p.105)

and Arnavon, in more recent times, has seen the encounter as little more than 'une entrée de cirque' (*35*, p.272). However, being the miser's first appearance on stage, this is a scene of particular importance in the structure of the comedy, and from the outset the audience is made aware of Harpagon's obsessive mistrust of his servant as he sees a scheming, pulsating life in his eyes and hands (199-202). Swift verbal exchanges interact with physical movement to capture the frantic indecision of the miser caught between two conflicting feelings of anger and suspicion, a desire to dominate and a fear of being duped; he first urges the servant out of his house and then holds him back:

HARPAGON: . . . Sors d'ici, encore une fois.
LA FLÈCHE: Hé bien! je sors.
HARPAGON: Attends. Ne m'emportes-tu rien? (220-22)

Set in this context, the miser's gesture, in its very absurdity, becomes the comic symbol of a febrile suspicion which does not recognise the bounds of normal perception and linguistic logic: for Harpagon, mistrust has become the only reality and even the evidence of his own eyes and senses is not sufficient to convince him of the servant's innocence:

HARPAGON: Montre-moi tes mains.
LA FLÈCHE: Les voilà.
HARPAGON: Les autres.
LA FLÈCHE: Les autres?
HARPAGON: Oui.
LA FLÈCHE: Les voilà. (224-29)

Through a careful patterning of the scene, Molière gives comic expression to the miser's gradual domination by the servant. Running through the encounter is the repeated exchange of mumbled aside and half-suspecting accusation. After his first curse, the cornered servant succeeds deftly in changing the subject (190-91). A few lines later the pattern is repeated as La Flèche murmers again to himself: 'Ah! qu'un homme comme cela mériterait bien ce qu'il craint, et que j'aurais de joie à le voler!' (236-37), but when questioned he avoids disclosure by replacing the incriminating word 'voler' in an innocent sentence: 'Je dis que vous fouillez bien partout pour voir si je vous ai volé' (241-42). Immediately afterwards, however, La Flèche goes further and exclaims: 'La peste soit de l'avarice et des avaricieux' (244). The now familiar and expected pattern of enquiry and hesitation is reproduced, but on this occasion Molière transforms the outcome; instead of concocting a lie, La Flèche defiantly repeats the phrase which the old man had only half heard. From a defensive position, the servant suddenly forces Harpagon back on himself, exploiting the ambiguous position of the miser who is conscious of his reputation and yet fears to admit it, and impelling him closer and closer to self-accusation:

> HARPAGON: De qui veux-tu parler?
> LA FLÈCHE: Des avaricieux.
> HARPAGON: Et qui sont-ils, ces avaricieux?
> LA FLÈCHE: Des vilains et des ladres.
> HARPAGON: Mais qui est-ce que tu entends par là?
> LA FLÈCHE: De quoi vous mettez-vous en peine?
> HARPAGON: Je me mets en peine de ce qu'il faut.
> LA FLÈCHE: Est-ce que vous croyez que je veux parler de vous?
> HARPAGON: Je crois ce que je crois. (249-57)

In the course of the scene the slow transformation of the miser's gestures and language reflect the gradual exposure of his vulnerability: dominant questions become feeble asides, positive searching leads to a desperate attempt simply to be rid of the servant, powerful assertions are reduced to pleas for silence and finally to speechlessness from the miser himself:

> HARPAGON: Je te rosserai, si tu parles.
> LA FLÈCHE: Qui se sent morveux, qu'il se mouche.
> HARPAGON: Te tairas-tu?
> LA FLÈCHE: Oui, malgré moi.
> HARPAGON: Ha! ha! (265-69)

In this context the outbreaks of violence represent not so much a gratuitous farcical interlude, but the only remaining means of expression for the miser confronted with the inadequacy of language as a defence: when words fail, his only recourse is to silence and blows.

The same art of suggestion may be seen in that stylised, farcical incident of III, 7 when Cléante offers Mariane the gift of his father's diamond ring. Two extremes interact in this scene as Harpagon struggles against an imposed act of generosity as exaggerated in its liberality as his own instinct takes him in the direction of parsimony. In the physical confrontation of father and son is reflected the underlying moral conflict in which avarice generates prodigality and prodigality avarice, excess breeding excess. The result is an encounter which comically juxtaposes normality and abnormality, embodied not simply in the figures of youth and old man, but rather in the opposition of charade and truth, apparently frustrated generosity on the father's part and deferent pleas from the son barely masking Harpagon's increasing anger and Cléante's glee at his revenge:

HARPAGON, *à part*: Peste soit . . .
CLÉANTE: Le voilà qui se scandalise de votre refus.
HARPAGON, *bas à son fils*: Ah! traître!
CLÉANTE: Vous voyez qu'il se désespère.
HARPAGON, *bas à son fils, en le menaçant*: Bourreau que tu es!
CLÉANTE: Mon père, ce n'est pas ma faute. Je fais ce que je puis pour l'obliger à la garder, mais elle est obstinée.
        (1436-42)

The most striking example of comic stylisation exploited for more suggestive effect is the sustained misunderstanding of Harpagon and Valère in V, 3; the miser accuses his *intendant* of a theft tantamount to murder, 'l'action la plus noire, l'attentat le plus horrible qui jamais ait été commis' (1951-52), which the young lover believes to refer to his courtship of Elise. It is another scene which Molière developed from the *Aulularia* and which has been criticised for its artificiality.[13] For all its apparent *invraisemblance*, however, the misunderstanding is

---

[13] cf. D. Mornet, *Molière*, Connaissance des Lettres, 11, Paris: Boivin, 1943, p.138.

quite consistent with the characters as they have been presented
to the audience. It comes quite naturally to the miser to speak of
his money as if it were a person, using terms such as 'sang'
(1978) and 'entrailles' (1979); it comes equally naturally to the
précieux lover to speak of his beloved in terms of priceless
riches, 'biens' (1998) and 'trésor' (2005). Furthermore, Valère's
ready belief that Harpagon's furious recriminations and talk of
personal loss refer to Elise suggest not simply the misleading
nature of the miser's vocabulary but also his own preoccupation
with his love and the slightly uneasy conscience of one aware of
the deception he has committed; it is indeed part of the irony
inherent in the encounter that he should give himself away
without realising it. As for Harpagon, obsessed as he is with
money, he readily and constantly attributes his fixation to
others. The potential for such confusion has been apparent from
the outset; that it should take place underlines the depth of the
characters' respective obsessions.

But Molière extracts from the scene further comic
significance. The more ardently Valère expresses his attachment
to Elise, speaking of their 'foi mutuelle' (2010) and their resolve
to stay together until death (2016), the more astonished
Harpagon becomes, and as the scene reaches its climax, farcical
innuendo blends with a more probing revelation of character:

> HARPAGON: Hé! dis-moi donc un peu: tu n'y as point
> touché?
> VALÈRE: Moi, y toucher! Ah! vous lui faites tort, aussi bien
> qu'à moi . . . Tous mes désirs se sont bornés à jouir de sa
> vue, et rien de criminel n'a profané la passion que ses
> beaux yeux m'ont inspirée.
> HARPAGON, *à part*: Les beaux yeux de ma cassette! Il parle
> d'elle comme un amant d'une maîtresse. (2036-37,
>   2045-49)

Molière clearly delights here in bringing the *quiproquo* to the
very brink of disclosure, and yet, through this comedy, he
suggests also the ambiguous nature of the miser's fixation.
Harpagon believes Valère to be dominated by a peculiarly
passionate attachment to money, an attitude which he finds

absurd; and yet, fixed in the obsession which underlies this misunderstanding, he is unable to see the same absurdity in himself — lucidity and blindness, awareness of normality and autonomous folly exist side by side. What the dramatist uncovers in this scene, moralists of the time frequently identified as an essential trait in human nature:

Nous nous pardonnons tout, et rien aux autres hommes,
On se voit d'un autre œil qu'on ne voit son prochain.
(La Fontaine, 'La Besace')[14]

The exaggeration and *invraisemblance*, buffoonery and farce which are such a significant part of *L'Avare* and indeed of much of Molière's comedy awakened considerable criticism. For many commentators of the period, this kind of comic stylisation took him far from truth to nature, from 'le naturel'. Rapin was to ask whether comedy could or should accommodate what he called 'de plus grands traits' and 'des impressions plus fortes' (*16*, p.117). In his own answer to the question, he made a distinction between Plautus who was seen to use such distortion simply as a means of appealing to 'le peuple', and Terence who depicted vices 'sans les grossir et sans les augmenter', appealed to the 'honnêtes gens' and did not go beyond the 'bornes de la nature': Molière was seen to belong firmly to the Plautine tradition. And Bouhours, in the *Manière de bien penser*, had his character Eudoxe see in Harpagon's monologue just that kind of facile exaggeration which is intended simply to amuse the public: his desire to make an audience laugh would be declared to be quite incompatible with any insight into character:

Les pièces comiques dont le but est de faire rire le peuple, doivent être comme ces tableaux que l'on voit de loin, & où les figures sont plus grandes que le naturel . . .[15]

---

[14] cf. also La Bruyère, 'Des jugements', 72: 'Tel parle d'un autre et en fait un portrait affreux, qui ne voit pas qu'il se peint lui-même'.

[15] D. Bouhours, *La Manière de bien penser dans les ouvrages d'esprit: dialogues*, nouvelle édition, Paris: Brunet, 1715; Sussex Reprints, 3, Brighton, 1971, p.459.

Such criticism was countered by Molière throughout his career. Firstly, this style of comic writing clearly provided entertainment for the audience, an aim which was of paramount importance to him. Dorante's famous pronouncement in the *Critique de l'Ecole des femmes*, Sc. 6 has often been seen to reflect the dramatist's own views: 'Je voudrais bien savoir si la grande règle de toutes les règles n'est pas de plaire'. Indeed, references to some of the most stylised moments in the play (e.g. the repetition of 'sans dot' in I, 5 or Harpagon's astonished outburst 'les beaux yeux de ma cassette' in V, 4) in the letters of Madame de Sévigné suggest the extent to which they had become embedded in the public imagination. It is this acute theatrical sense which Grimarest would single out in his *Vie*:

> Molière connaissait déjà le point de vue du Théâtre, qui demande de gros traits pour affecter le Public; et ce principe lui a toujours réussi dans tous les caractères qu'il a voulu peindre. (*14*, p.48)

But more than this, Molière's particular comic style could be and was justified for its contribution to his wider purpose. In the *Critique de l'Ecole des femmes*, Sc.6, Dorante refers to the opening scene of *L'Ecole des femmes* where the hero Arnolphe, who seeks to create in Agnès a pliable wife for himself, enthusiastically recalls her innocence in asking him whether children are conceived through the ear; Dorante suggests that the incident provides more than just amusement at the expense of a naïve heroine, but serves to reveal the foolishness of Arnolphe who is so excited by it. Set in its context, the simple comic interlude becomes 'une chose qui caractérise l'homme et peint d'autant mieux son extravagance'. Similarly in the *Lettre sur l'Imposteur*, written in defence of *Tartuffe*, it is argued that the essence of Orgon's neglect of his family and fixation with a villainous *directeur de conscience* is captured perfectly in his constant and inapposite repetition of the question 'Et Tartuffe?', every time his servant tries to speak to him about his wife, this being seen as:

... la manière du monde la plus heureuse et la plus naturelle de produire un caractère aussi outré que celui de ce bon Seigneur, qui paraît de cette sorte d'abord dans le plus haut degré de son entêtement . . . (see *1*, I, p.1152)

Other early critics of *L'Avare* appreciated this. An incident noted by Monchesnay in his *Bolaeana* (1742) records how Boileau laughed throughout a performance of *L'Avare*, and yet praised it for avoiding vulgar exaggeration:

M. Despréaux préférait *L'Avare* de Molière à celui de Plaute, qui est outré dans plusieurs endroits et entre dans des détails bas et ridicules. Au contraire celui du Comique moderne est dans la nature, et une des meilleures pièces de l'auteur . . . (see *15*, I, p.318)

The attribution of the remark to Boileau may be uncertain, but the analysis itself remains valid, and it finds an echo in Riccoboni's commentary on the same play:

tout y est si ingénieusement amené, que le Comique s'y présente naturellement à chaque instant, & se trouve à la portée de tous les spectateurs, parce qu'il est tiré du fonds de la chose même, ou du ridicule du caractère. (*17*, p.262)

Both judgements rightly stress the particular quality of Molière's art, immediate in its comic appeal yet probing in its implications. For this dramatist, indeed, the twin aims of *plaire* and *instruire* are not mutually exclusive but suggestively interdependent. The most elementary forms of comedy may in certain contexts convey more subtle insights, *invraisemblance* may express truth. The physical jostling of III, 7, or the ludicrous misunderstanding of V, 3, the mechanically repeated courtesies of 1, 4, or the miser's grasping of his own arm in IV, 7, all reflect this curious paradox, being incidents which provide enjoyment but which also in their different ways 'caractérisent l'homme' and suggest the nature of an obsession, an *extravagance*. Equally significant, however, is the fact that these critics, like Molière himself, stress that such a comic style is 'natural'. For Molière, here as elsewhere, to be 'natural' is not necessarily to reproduce reality, but to reveal it: and seen from this perspective, the stylisation, exaggeration and disproportion which inspire laughter become not simply an adjunct of the play's main purpose but an integral part of it.

5. *Structure and Unity*

L'ordonnance de ses comédies est toujours défectueuse en quelque chose, et
ses dénouements ne sont point heureux.
(16, p.121)

The structure of *L'Avare* is often seen as loose and episodic,
awkwardly juxtaposing romance and farce, the fantastical and
the everyday, and the conclusion has been drawn that the play is
simply a series of largely unconnected comic sketches centring
on Harpagon. For those who conceive the comedy in this way,
the romantic elements, particularly those in Act I, appear quite
incongruous. For Arnavon, the opening scene 'repousse
terriblement' *(35*, p.262), Sarcey describes the exposition as
'pénible' and 'entortillée' *(19*, II, p.128) and Descotes speaks of
complete excisions of the first two scenes in certain stage
productions *(23*, p.133). Other critics, however, find in this
romantic dimension a crucial dramatic function. For some it is a
refreshing corrective to what is seen as the otherwise horrifying
picture of the miser and his vice and offers a comforting
suggestion of normality. In his edition of the text, Dullin
underlines the importance of this 'arrière-plan lumineux de
jeunesse et de fraîcheur' *(4*, p.18) and, for Adam, the whole
unity and meaning of the play derives from the adventures of the
lovers: 'Elles lui donnent sa résonance, sa gravité, sa
signification humaine' *(20*, III, p.373). For Peacock *(46)*, on the
other hand, the opening scenes establish an atmosphere of
fantasy and theatricality which enables the audience to keep in
perspective the comedy which follows.

The juxtaposition of characters and tones is clearly an
essential part of the play's comic structure, as has been seen
already in the various intrigues which in their different ways
oppose the lovers and the miser; similar contrasts with
Harpagon are implied in the presentation of Anselme. Both old
men are seen to contemplate marriage with a younger girl, but

Anselme, unlike Harpagon, clearly does not automatically
assume that he is loved: his insight in the final act contrasts
markedly with the miser's absurd self-indulgence: 'Ce n'est pas
mon dessein de me faire épouser par force et de rien prétendre à
un cœur qui se serait donné' (2118-19) and intensifies
Harpagon's comic force as a lover. This contrast is reflected also
in the relationship which each is seen to have with his son. In
V, 5 Valère and Anselme learn each other's true identity. In this
traditional scene of recognition, apparent conflict soon dissolves
into harmony, and when the son discovers his father, incredulity
merges with inexpressible joy:

> VALÈRE: Vous êtes notre père?
> MARIANE: C'est vous que ma mère a tant pleuré?
> ANSELME: Oui, ma fille, oui, mon fils, je suis Don Thomas
>   d'Alburcy, que le Ciel garantit des ondes . . . (2207-10)

In contrast, the meeting of Cléante and Harpagon in II, 2
parodies the familiar conventional pattern. In this scene, father
and son seek not to disclose but to conceal who they really are,
and when finally they are brought face to face, they are filled not
with delight but with irritation and astonishment:

> HARPAGON: Comment! pendard, c'est toi qui t'aban-
>   donnes à ces coupables extrémités?
> CLÉANTE: Comment! mon père, c'est vous qui vous portez
>   à ces honteuses actions! (740-43)

Revelations about identity do not here resolve conflict but
aggravate it: the traditional sequence of events in the final scenes
underlines the extent of this earlier deviation from it.

The comic structure of the play, however, is not simply based
on the juxtaposition of flexibility and rigidity, enlightened
common sense and blindness implied in these examples. Among
the characters themselves who stand in opposition to the miser,
certain contrasting pairings are evident. Cléante and Valère, for
instance, are never in close contact with each other, but, in the
opening scenes particularly, contrasts are implied between the

two lovers, each faced with potential trouble from Harpagon. Valère has many qualities of the hero of tragi-comedy, of uncertain birth and actively engaged in winning his lady; Cléante, on the other hand, is constantly thwarted in the heroic quest he would wish to pursue, rooted to banal reality by his need for money. Valère has rescued his beloved from a shipwreck, Cléante cannot even afford to offer financial aid; Valère confidently seeks to control his fate, Cléante is uncertain and frustrated, seeing himself as the victim both of his father and of his 'mauvaise destinée' (IV, 1, 1493). This juxtaposition of the two lovers lends considerable force to the comic presentation of Cléante, the would-be hero, but it does more than this. Divergences between the two characters suggest contrasting sides of the miser's nature; in Valère Harpagon sees all that he would wish to be — the self-assured defender of a philosophy which gives respectability to frugal living —, and in Cléante, he finds all that he dislikes and fears — extravagance, expense and the threat to his authority.

Maître Jacques and La Flèche are also contrasted throughout the comedy. It is something of a comic tradition to oppose the wily and the foolish servant, the guile and skill of the one throwing into relief the awkwardness of the other: the confidence of La Flèche underlines Maître Jacques's timorousness, as the one enjoys taunting the miser and the other succeeds only in finding himself trouble. Each has his own contrasting attitude to Harpagon: La Flèche stresses his inhumanity and moral guilt ('je croirais, en le volant, faire une action méritoire', 710), Maître Jacques suggests the affection which he nevertheless evokes ('je me sens pour vous de la tendresse, en dépit que j'en aie; et, après mes chevaux, vous êtes la personne que j'aime le plus', 1186-88); one sets out to outwit, the other to enlighten. Here again this contrast reflects different qualities in the central figure. La Flèche with his challenging insolence first brings out into the open Harpagon's fear of being robbed and it is significantly through this servant that the miser's self-fulfilling phobia is realised. Maître Jacques, on the other hand, suggests in his own double act of *cocher* and *cuisinier*, undertaken with a mixture of pride and incompetence, the tension between parsimony and concern for his reputation which characterises Harpagon, and his merely temporary success in 'resolving' the quarrel between father and son as he glosses over quite clear disagreement with talk of sound sense mirrors the fragility of the miser's protestations of confidence and control.

This use of contrast to reveal different facets of the central character extends also to contrasts of scenes. Some examples of this have been discussed already — the two incidents in which Harpagon is confronted with his reputation (I, 3 and III, 1), the first one imposed, the second solicited, reflect again the complex blend of rejection and fear in the miser's attitude to the outside world; and the two scenes of recognition (II, 2 and V, 5) suggestively juxtapose two relationships of father and son, the one traditional, the other a comic deviation from it. At two strategic points in the comedy (I, 4 and IV, 3) Harpagon questions Cléante about his opinion of Mariane. In I, 4, his enquiry, in all its apparent sanity, elicits enthusiastic responses from his son:

HARPAGON: Comment, mon fils, trouvez-vous cette fille?
CLÉANTE: Une fort charmante personne.
HARPAGON: Sa physionomie?
CLÉANTE: Toute honnête et pleine d'esprit.
HARPAGON: Son air et sa manière?
CLÉANTE: Admirables, sans doute. (392-97)

The audience, like Cléante, is deceived by Harpagon's language, but what at first appeared to be good-humoured concern for his son is subsequently revealed to be the ultimate expression of his obsession. So natural does it seem to the miser to take the fair Mariane for himself and to marry his son to a financially attractive widow, that he can speak of such proposals as if they were quite normal: 'vous n'aurez ni l'un ni l'autre aucun lieu de vous plaindre de tout ce que je prétends faire' (385-86). It is in contrast with this scene that the implications of the second conversation are fully revealed. Once again, Harpagon is heard to speak the language of normality, but on this occasion his deliberate intention to deceive his son is made plain:

> HARPAGON: Ô çà, intérêt de belle-mère à part, que te
> semble, à toi, de cette personne?
> CLÉANTE: Ce qui m'en semble?
> HARPAGON: Oui, de son air, de sa taille, de sa beauté, de
> son esprit.
> CLÉANTE: Là, là.
> HARPAGON: Mais encore?
> CLÉANTE: A vous en parler franchement, je ne l'ai pas
> trouvée ici ce que je l'avais crue. Son air est de franche
> coquette; sa taille est assez gauche, sa beauté très
> médiocre, et son esprit des plus communs. (1580-90)

This evident echo of the earlier scene increases the comic force
of the encounter as Cléante is seen now rather unconvincingly to
take back all his previous opinions about Mariane, and is led
slowly towards inept self-disclosure. However, the contrast of
Harpagon's two bouts of sanity, the one seemingly unconscious,
the other calculating, focuses attention also on the miser himself
and on the paradox of an obsession in which apparent
imperviousness to the values of others cannot disguise his acute
awareness of them.

This paradox is made all the more suggestive by the further
parallels implied between this scene and I, 5 in which Valère and
Harpagon also discuss the principles underlying marriage.
Significantly, when the miser deceives his son by his assumption
of an enlightened attitude to marriage, he brings forward many
of the proposals which Valère had used — to no avail — against
him. The young hero's praise of fathers who seek in partners for
their children 'cette douce conformité qui sans cesse y maintient
l'honneur, la tranquillité et la joie' (522-23), is reflected in
Harpagon's opening: 'j'ai songé qu'on pourra trouver à redire
de me voir marier à une si jeune personne' (1600-01); just as the
lover had argued that happiness in marriage must be based on
'inclination':

> . . . il faudrait au moins quelque temps pour voir si son
> inclination pourra s'accommoder avec . . . il y va d'être

heureux ou malheureux toute sa vie . . . (493-94, 505-06)

Harpagon makes quite explicit the same link: 'un mariage ne saurait être heureux où l'inclination n'est pas' (1616-17); and Valère's argument that disproportion in age could lead to 'des accidents très fâcheux' (514-15), is repeated by the miser, conscious of 'des suites fâcheuses, où je n'ai garde de me commettre' (1621-22). Rigidity contrasts with guile, unconscious mania with self-conscious calculation as one scene echoes another; through them is suggested again the complex force of avarice in which confidence and suspicion merge and conflict.

Molière's use of contrast is most significantly apparent in the play's double ending. The events of the final act have been seen as an absurd intrusion of fantasy, having little bearing on the development and resolution of the plot. The family links which bind Anselme, Mariane and Valère are revealed in a sequence of recognitions which carry all the marks of Plautine comedy or the romantic tragi-comedy, so popular a generation before Molière; shipwrecks and abductions, separation and survival all have their part to play in this richly coloured narration. An atmosphere of wonderment is created, clearly expressed by the astonished and overjoyed Anselme:

> Ô Ciel, quels sont les traits de ta puissance! et que tu fais bien voir qu'il n'appartient qu'à toi de faire des miracles!
> (2203-04)

Such revelations have been seen to indicate Molière's excessive love of the romanesque,[16] his shameless optimism (*39*, p.17) or simply his hurried, flawed construction of the play. Critics writing shortly after the dramatist's death commonly regarded his denouements as unsatisfactory and the tradition is still alive in more recent times (cf. *3*, p.xliii).

The very self-conscious excess of the fantasy suggests, however, an element of literary parody notable already in Molière's work. In his early play *L'Etourdi*, Mascarille plans

[16] e.g. E. Rigal, *Molière*, 2 vols, Paris: Hachette, 1908, II, p.161.

happiness for his master in IV, 1 by engineering the kind of involved discoveries frequent, he claims, in real life:

> C'est qu'en fait d'aventure il est très ordinaire
> De voir gens pris sur mer par quelque Turc corsaire,
> Puis être à leur famille à point nommé rendus,
> Après quinze ou vingt ans qu'on les a cru perdus,
>
> (1335-38)

and in *Les Précieuses ridicules*, Sc. 4, Magdelon tells her father that true love is not possible if one has not first lived through a sequence of exciting romantic adventures:

> Mon père, voilà ma cousine qui vous dira, aussi bien que moi, que le mariage ne doit jamais arriver qu'après les autres aventures.

Bearing so clearly the marks of a well-known but outmoded literary tradition, this intrusion of the fantastic into the ending of *L'Avare* has its own comic force, its theatricality thrown into relief by the unromantic domesticity of the miser's household. But the function of this contrast extends further than such comic pastiche. The miraculous events themselves prefigure the same pattern of events which characterise Harpagon's own fate, and reflect the nature of his obsession. For both old men, treasured possessions thought lost are unexpectedly recovered, and just as Valère and Mariane find in their father their true identity, Harpagon finds in his *cassette* the money which defines him. In this ironical juxtaposition of fantasy and banality, the improbable world of the theatre is punctured by, and yet reveals, the world of the miser.

Significantly, though, this internally contrasting ending itself stands in contrast with another ending, sketched out by Frosine in IV, 1. The plan proposed by the servant suggests the final duping of the hero, a triumph over his avarice:

> . . . si nous avions quelque femme un peu sur l'âge qui fût de mon talent et jouât assez bien pour contrefaire une

dame de qualité . . . j'aurais assez d'adresse pour faire
accroire à votre père que ce serait une personne riche, outre
ses maisons, de cent mille écus en argent comptant.
                                                    (1541-42, 1545-47)

Such a proposal has a primary comic force of course, insofar as
it originates with a schemer who has already failed so dismally to
outwit the miser; Frosine's brash confidence is ironically out of
place. But it is also important in that it suggests a ruse which will
lead in some way to the victim's understanding of the gullibility
to which his avarice gives rise:

. . . quand, ébloui de ce leurre, il aurait une fois consenti à
ce qui vous touche, il importerait peu ensuite qu'il se
désabusât, en venant à vouloir voir clair aux effets de notre
marquise. (1551-54)

This outcome, familiar in comedy since the *Miles gloriosus* of
Plautus, is quite different from the events of Act V as they turn
out. It is a disparity which is often singled out as another feature
of the play's defective construction, and yet such deviations
from tradition are essential to the comic structure. Indeed,
Frosine's forgotten scheme is just one of several echoes of the
conventional denouement scattered at various points in the text
but which are not taken up in the final scenes. The warm
welcome of a father to his new son-in-law is prefigured in the
miser's praise of Valère, 'le brave garçon' (581) at the height of
his naïvety in I, 5, but is conspicuously absent at the end;
forgiveness of a disobedient son is parodied in the mistaken
reconciliation of IV, 5, but not reproduced; and apparent insight
into his foolishness forms part of the miser's elaborate charade
of IV, 3, but never materialises again. Traditional elements are
clearly present in the comedy and yet inserted out of place,
unfinished, as part of a misunderstanding: against this
background the actual denouement, in all its departures from
convention, is thrown into relief.
    It is this constant interaction of contrasts and parallels which
is perhaps the most striking feature of the play's structure.

Characters are important not simply in the context of their own particular intrigues but in the light they shed on each other or on the different facets of Harpagon's avarice, and scenes acquire additional significance as part of a comic network of themes and variations. Such a structure creates links between apparently disparate episodes, but in its suggestion of a world where characters both underline and reflect the miser's obsession, and in its constant juxtaposition of tradition and distortion, it implies a particularly complex moral vision which must now be investigated.

6. Comedy and Morality

> . . . qui peut disconvenir aussi que le
> Théâtre de ce même Molière . . . ne soit
> une école de vices et de mauvaises mœurs.
> (*18*, p.45)

The link between comedy and the presentation of sound morality was, in theoretical pronouncements, quite clear. In the *Epître liminaire* (1579) to his collected plays, for instance, the Renaissance dramatist Larivey saw comedy as 'une morale philosophie, donnant lumière à toute honneste discipline' (see *32*, p.197), and for Rapin, writing a century later, the aims of the genre were unequivocal:

> . . . sa fin est de montrer sur le théâtre les défauts des particuliers, pour guérir les défauts du public, et de corriger le peuple par la crainte d'estre moqué. (*16*, p.114)

Molière has often been portrayed as the castigator of wrong. At the time of his death, Robinet lamented the passing of:

> Ce comique chrétien, ce grand peintre des mœurs,
> De qui les âpres vers et la mordante prose
> Des défauts de son temps furent les vrais censeurs
> (*Lettre en vers*, 25.2.1673; see *15*, II, p.445)

Meredith saw him wielding a 'shrieking . . . scourge upon vice';[17] and in his edition of *L'Avare*, Wilson sees the dramatist setting out 'to expose another of mankind's moral sores' (*3*, p.xxvi). Molière's own comments on the subject, particularly those which answer criticism of his earlier *Tartuffe*, are well known, and in his *Premier placet au Roi* he makes plain a connection between comedy and moral correction:

[17] G. Meredith, *An Essay on Comedy and the Uses of the Comic Spirit* (1897); ed. L. Cooper, New York: Kennikat, 1972, p.96.

> Le devoir de la comédie étant de corriger les hommes en les divertissant, j'ai cru que, dans l'emploi où je me trouve, je n'avais rien de mieux à faire que d'attaquer par des peintures ridicules les vices de mon siècle.

How far the sustained and violent attack on *Tartuffe* led him to distort his views on the nature and intentions of comedy may be widely debated. One point, though, is clear. If any moral purpose is to be served by comedy, it is not through preaching but by exposing the absurdity of certain attitudes or forms of behaviour. Indeed, it is seen as part of comedy's insight into character that this approach is ultimately more effective than any explicit moral address. Nothing, Molière argues in his *Préface* to the same comedy *Tartuffe*, is more stinging than ridicule:

> C'est une grande atteinte aux vices que de les exposer à la risée de tout le monde. On souffre aisément des répréhensions; mais on ne souffre point la raillerie. On veut bien être méchant, mais on ne veut point être ridicule.

The absence of direct moralising is clear in *L'Avare*, and comparison with other seventeenth-century writers reveals this quite sharply. Analysis of the usury scene has shown how Molière deliberately plays down the potential for explicit moral debate in Boisrobert's confrontation; and nowhere in the presentation of Harpagon is there to be found the same kind of unequivocal condemnation seen in La Bruyère's presentation of the 'âmes sales, pétries de boue et d'ordure' ('Des biens de fortune', 58) or in Boileau's picture of Tardieu 'à pied dans les ruisseaux traînant l'ignominie' (Satire X). In the comic context Molière's characters are examined not against a standard of absolute moral worth, but against a standard of normality, dictated by custom, nature and reason. In the *Lettre sur l'Imposteur*, the author makes this particularly telling analysis:

> Le ridicule est donc la forme extérieure et sensible que la providence de la nature a attachée à tout ce qui est

déraisonnable . . . (see *1*, p.1174)

In the potentially reprehensible or repellent character of the miser Molière clearly uncovers the comic incongruities in behaviour which, on a social level, lead to absurd excentricities, and, on a human level, reveal a fruitless search for fulfilment and stability. Indeed, Perrault, writing shortly after the creation of *L'Avare*, contrasted with evident approval the life and penetration of Molière's comedy with the general moralising on the subject of avarice in Horace's 1st Satire. He saw in the Roman poet:

> . . . des réflexions morales contre les avares, bien vagues & bien communes. *L'Avare* de Molière est bien d'un autre sel & d'une autre vivacité.[18]

And yet, *L'Avare* was not immune to criticisms of immorality. The basis for these, however, was not imputed ribaldry and unseemly innuendo, as had been the case with *L'Ecole des femmes*; in this respect, *L'Avare* is, by the standards of farce, particularly chaste in its presentation of young lovers and lecherous old men. In this instance, the criticism penetrated further to the attitudes and behaviour of the characters themselves. Riccoboni mentioned widespread criticism of Cléante, whose lack of respect for his father was thought of as particularly shocking:

> On censure dans *Cléante*, fils d'Harpagon, le peu de respect qu'il a pour son père; on trouve qu'en cela les mœurs & les bienséances sont trop blessées . . . & qu'un pareil caractère pourroit diminuer dans un fils qui verroit la représentation de *l'Avare* les sentiments de respect qu'il doit à son père . . . (*17*, pp.255-56)

and Rousseau, writing later in the eighteenth century, saw the intrigues of this character as profoundly disturbing, eclipsing the

18 Ch. Perrault, *Parallèle des Anciens et des Modernes en ce qui regarde les arts et les sciences*, 4 vols, Paris: J.-B. Coignard & Fils, 1692-96, III, p.225.

immorality of the miser himself:

> C'est un grand vice d'être avare et de prêter à usure; mais n'en est-ce pas un plus grand encore à un fils de voler son père, de lui manquer de respect, de lui faire mille insultants reproches . . .? (*18*, p.47)

Cléante's comic retort to his father in their argument of IV, 5 was regarded as all the more worrying as the dramatist seemingly solicits the audience's sympathy for the young man:

> Si la plaisanterie est excellente, en est-elle moins punissable? et la pièce où l'on fait aimer le fils insolent qui l'a faite, en est-elle moins une école de mauvaises mœurs?
> (*18*, p.47)

The same line of approach was taken in the next century by Dumas in his notes to *Le Fils naturel*. He too argued that Harpagon deserves punishment, but that Cléante's resort to theft in order to administer 'cette justice arbitraire' was even more reprehensible; this critic would have much preferred to see the son earn the money necessary to marry Mariane by finding a worthy job and setting a good example:

> Molière eût pu être ainsi tout aussi écrivain, tout aussi observateur, tout aussi intéressant, tout aussi amusant, tout aussi moraliste, en devenant plus *moralisateur* et plus *utile*.[19]

Knutson's more recent assessment of Cléante as 'the bad son [who] carries rebellion to the moral limits of comedy' (*29*, p.97) falls very much in this same critical tradition. Nor is it only Cléante who was criticised for immoral behaviour. Although exonerating this character on the grounds of reasonable self-defence, Riccoboni remained worried by the deceit practised by Valère and Elise:

---

[19] A. Dumas, *Théâtre complet*, VIII (1886); in Alsip, *34*, p.102.

Valère . . . ne se conduit pas d'une manière convenable, &
. . . il passe les bornes de la bienséance . . . Elise d'un autre
côté, en lui permettant de faire cette supposition à son
père, manque aux bonnes mœurs & à la bienséance; &
jamais l'on ne doit exposer de pareils modèles aux yeux du
Spectateur . . . (*17*, p. 253-54)

and Gaxotte, more recently, has been led to see in the comedy
the presentation of a 'jeunesse . . . flétrie' (*26*, p.287; cf. also *38*,
p.206).

Such criticisms as these suggest on one level a deliberate or
unconscious ignorance of the dramatist's comic angle of vision.
Ruse and guile are often essential to the plots of comedy and do
not in themselves imply moral flaws. Indeed, in a world where
wit, energy and youth frequently overcome the inflexibility of
age and avarice, the old are seen to deserve their fate; their
susceptibility to trickery is both the reflection of and the
punishment for their particular moral short-sightedness. In
L'Ecole des maris (II, 1) Isabelle confidently justifies her
planned deception of her jealous guardian, acknowledging that
it is a 'projet bien hardi', but adding that his 'injuste rigueur'
wholly vindicates her; equally in Boisrobert's *La Belle Plaideuse*
(V, 3), the miser is seen to be the cause of his own, much
deserved downfall:

L'avarice vous perd; quand un fils misérable
Ne vole que son père, il n'est pas si coupable.

(*6*, p.578)

In *L'Avare*, the tricksters defend themselves on similar grounds
for the plots they hatch against Harpagon: he has brought such
scheming on himself. Valère's remarks in the opening scene of
the comedy:

l'excès de son avarice et la manière austère dont il vit avec
ses enfants pourraient autoriser des choses plus étranges

(61-63)

are to a large extent echoed by Cléante who laments the atmosphere of 'rigoureuse épargne' (163) and the 'sécheresse étrange' (164) inflicted on them, and again by La Flèche in II, 1, for whom the miser's excesses turn the crime of theft into a virtue: 'il me donnerait, par ses procédés, des tentations de voler, et je croirais, en le volant, faire une action méritoire' (709-10). Nevertheless, for all its similarities with this comic tradition, *L'Avare* does in certain respects diverge from it and in ways which suggest a particularly acute probing of the moral problem posed by avarice.

Unlike conventional heroes who happily accept the ethic of deception, for instance, Valère himself is shown to be slightly uneasy in his own self-defence of I, 1:

> La sincérité souffre un peu au métier que je fais; mais quand on a besoin des hommes, il faut bien s'ajuster à eux.
>
> (85-86)

Mariane, equally, is quite unable to accept the full implications of Frosine's schemes, when the servant argues that marriage to the financially, if not physically desirable, old man will certainly be very brief (III, 4, 1290-94). For the young and fair Dorimène in Molière's early farcical comedy *Le Mariage forcé*, Sc.7, the prospect of a substantial inheritance is more than adequate incentive to tolerate a temporary inconvenience:

> J'ai embrassé cette occasion-ci de me mettre à mon aise, et je l'ai fait sur l'espérance de me voir bientôt délivrée du barbon que je prends.

Mariane, however, cannot react in this way; she reflects instead on the curious moral ambiguity of such a proposal, standing aside from the smooth and traditional comic movement to see the plot in a quite new and unexpected way:

> Mon Dieu! Frosine, c'est une étrange affaire lorsque, pour être heureuse, il faut souhaiter ou attendre le trépas de quelqu'un . . . (1295-96)

Furthermore, in the structure of the comedy, certain similarities are suggested between the apparently different characters and values of young and old. Valère's passion is no less absolute, nor his language less hyperbolic than the miser's. For the youthful hero, to lose Elise's trust is tantamount to being murdered: 'Ne m'assassinez point . . . par les sensibles coups d'un soupçon outrageux' (29-30), just as, for Harpagon, the same effect derives from loss of his wealth: 'Je suis perdu, je suis assassiné' (1808); for Valère, precaution which stands in his way is 'fâcheuse' (29), just as for the miser opposition may lead to anger; and in consecutive scenes each reacts with blows to the 'impertinence' of Maître Jacques (III, 1 and III, 2). Both Elise and her father are seen to have the same capacity for stubborn assertion in I, 4, and between the miser and his son a wide range of suggestive parallels is implied.

Both Harpagon and Cléante see similar qualities in Mariane. The son's early effusions of I, 2 in which he extols in her 'une douceur pleine d'attraits, une bonté toute engageante, une honnêteté adorable' (145-46), are echoed within two scenes by the miser himself in an albeit drier style: 'son maintien honnête et sa douceur m'ont gagné l'âme' (416); both exhibit the same impatience in their courtship and Cléante's eager question to La Flèche in II, 1: 'Comment va notre affaire? Les choses pressent plus que jamais' (589-90), is mirrored exactly by Harpagon in II, 5 to Frosine (842). Equally, they share the same desire for secrecy, the same sense of urgency, La Flèche telling his young master with some surprise that the mysterious usurer 'apporte encore plus de soin à se cacher que vous' (617-18), and Cléante, no less than Harpagon, leaps to the conclusion that he has been betrayed in moments of crisis: 'Lui aurait-on appris qui je suis? et serais-tu pour me trahir?' (730-31). Both father and son share the same fondness for violent outbursts: when Cléante finds his desires thwarted by the usurer's terms, he curses in frustration: 'Que la peste l'étouffe avec sa discrétion, le traître, le bourreau qu'il est' (688-89), oaths which the miser echoes when he finds himself the victim of his son's extravagance in III, 7: 'Peste soit . . . Ah! traître! . . . Bourreau que tu es!' (1436, 1438, 1440). And it is not without significance that both

Harpagon and his son express within four scenes of each other in Act II the joy they feel at apparently successful plotting and their desire to outlive each other: Cléante's frustrated outburst in II, 1: 'on s'étonne, après cela, que les fils souhaitent qu'ils meurent' (701-02), is followed by Harpagon's curt 'Tant mieux' (842) in response to Frosine's remark that the miser will survive even his grandchildren.

Cléante, as has been seen, is no less irritated than the miser himself at the thought of being thwarted in his schemes, and there is in both characters a certain fixation with their own world. Just as Harpagon can say in V, 4: 'Non, non, je ne veux rien entendre' (2100), Cléante openly tells his sister in I, 2 that he will not listen to anything he does not want to, 'car enfin mon amour ne veut rien écouter' (118). Cléante indeed is able to mimic the language of his father, as aware as Harpagon of others' views and as resolved to ignore them when it suits his purpose:

> Je sais que je dépends d'un père, et que le nom de fils me soumet à ses volontés . . . qu'il en faut plutôt croire les lumières de leur prudence que l'aveuglement de notre passion; et que l'emportement de la jeunesse nous entraîne le plus souvent dans des précipices fâcheux . . .
>
> (106-08, 113-16)

Such parallels as these have a certain comic effect as the old man is seen to distort attributes of the young — and vice versa — but they are characteristic on a more general level of the suggestive interaction of the two seemingly distinct sets of values. It is against this background that the complex force of the *comédie d'intrigue* may be seen with its profusion of disguise and impersonation.

The simple juxtaposition of young and old which begins the comedy, where the *précieux* effusions of the lovers contrast with the concrete brutish vocabulary of the miser, gradually dissolves in the course of the play. The language and attitudes of the miser are to be found equally in the mouths of Valère, Cléante and Frosine; the language and attitudes of the young find expression also in Harpagon. Valère is able to imitate the miser, cajoling him with talk of unconditional filial obedience ('la grande raison de *sans dot*', 555-56) and of honourable parsimony ('il faut que la frugalité règne dans les repas qu'on donne', 1125-26) and Frosine confidently echoes the old man's scorn of the young with her own talk of 'beaux morveux' (939) and 'jeunes blondins' (945-46). Harpagon equally can deceive his children as he speaks of parental affection ('vous n'aurez ni l'un ni l'autre aucun lieu de vous plaindre de tout ce que je prétends faire', 385-86) or enlightenment ('je suis plus raisonnable que tu ne penses. Je ne veux point forcer ton inclination', 1612-13). Such parallels as these suggest a structure which does not simply oppose normal and abnormal, romantic and prosaic, but confronts irreconcilable opponents, each committed with equal rigidity to his personal vision. The ability of both miser and lovers to imitate each other reflects not understanding and flexibility but, paradoxically, their unshiftable desire to further their own ends. Not surprisingly, apparent similarity of language can only lead to misunderstanding and confusion, and the characters can communicate with each other no better at the end of the play than they could at the beginning. The schemers gain little from their impersonation of the miser; and Harpagon himself can neither tame nor escape from the outside world which they represent.

The result is a suggestive impasse which the fantasy of the denouement may end, but does not resolve. Unlike the lovers in many other comedies of the period, these couples are not united because of the convincing force of their passion or their own manipulative skills — as Valère had earlier proposed — but as the result of a remarkable sequence of chance survivals and coincidental meetings. Furthermore, this 'success' implies no triumph over the miser who has threatened them throughout the play. Although two father figures are opposed in the plot, one is not now proved right and the other wrong, as is the case at the end of *L'Ecole des maris* where the educational theories of the misguided Sganarelle are shown to be quite inadequate, and his defeat at the hands of the wily lovers is seen as an appropriate punishment by Ariste (III, 9):

> D'une telle action vos procédés sont cause;
> Et je vois votre sort malheureux à ce point
> Que, vous sachant dupé, l'on ne vous plaindra point.

Instead, as was seen in the previous chapter, a clear parallel is suggested between the fate of the two old men, both reunited with what they hold most dear. Harpagon is not reformed like La Fontaine's *enfouisseur*, 'résolu de jouir/Plus n'entasser, plus n'enfouir' ('L'Enfouisseur et son compère'), nor does he happily accept that he has been outwitted, like Gorgibus in *Le Médecin volant*, Sc.15:

> Je vous pardonne, et suis heureusement trompé par Sganarelle, ayant un si brave gendre.

The miser may frequently bring trouble on himself, but he is finally left untouchable in his own world, maintaining his avarice in all its ambiguity as he contemplates wearing a new suit at his children's wedding, provided that Anselme will pay for it (2264-65). The resultant ending is not one of harmony but of fragmentation, as each father expresses personal happiness and leaves the stage to a different destination:

> ANSELME: Allons vite faire part de notre joie à votre mère.
> HARPAGON: Et moi, voir ma chère cassette. (2281-82)

Earlier critics suggested that the 'immorality' of the play derives from Molière's apparent favouring of the young in his granting success to their ruses; his boldness, however, resides in the very absence of such a simple solution. Instead of following a conventional comic pattern of youth overcoming old age, he creates instead an ending where tradition and deviation from it are starkly juxtaposed: the children find happiness, but it comes by chance, self-consciously theatrical in its excess, and without reconciliation; the miser's plans are foiled, but he is unchanged, unrepentant and isolated. The result is a comedy in which the audience is invited not so much to improve itself, to be shocked by, or scornful of, the miser — or his children — but to reflect on the nature of an obsession and its far-reaching consequences; not to reconstruct a picture of man as he should be in a perfect world, but to see him as he is in this one. Harpagon's joy at the end of this familiar comic plot of scheming and ridicule stands as a suggestive counterbalance to the traditional theory that comedy can correct, and reflects the penetrating observation of Béralde in Molière's last comedy, *Le Malade imaginaire* (III, 3), who remarks on the ultimate ineffectiveness of trying to change human nature:

> . . . à regarder les choses en philosophe, je ne vois point de plus plaisante momerie, je ne vois rien de plus ridicule qu'un homme qui se veut mêler d'en guérir un autre.

The ending of the comedy, like the comedy itself, does not carry answers and moral judgements but offers food for thought.

Conclusion

> Un Ouvrage aussi singulier & aussi
> difficile, car je suis presque certain qu'il
> a plus coûté à Molière que deux
> Comédies de son invention, mérite
> l'attention, & même l'admiration des
> connoisseurs. (*17*, pp.186-87)

In spite of its evident popularity in the theatre, *L'Avare* is often singled out among Molière's comedies as being particularly bleak in its substance and impact. Gutwirth sees it as 'probably Molière's harshest play' (*43*, p.359) and Gaxotte as 'la plus dure, la plus ingrate, la plus aride' (*26*, p.286) in the dramatist's output. Although the play's comic force is rather more sophisticated than such terms suggest, it is clear that as a comedy it does differ from many of Molière's other mature works in certain significant respects.

The relationship of father and son, for instance, is more complex here than in any other comedy of Molière. In the *Fourberies de Scapin*, Octave is very much the timid son of classical comic tradition who trembles to oppose his father, and in other comedies any rifts between the generations lead inevitably to reconciliations; in *Tartuffe*, for example, Orgon may dispossess and curse his son, but by the final act Damis has returned and willingly defends his abused father against the usurper. In *L'Avare*, however, Cléante is much more impulsive and uncompromising, similar indeed to Harpagon himself. There may be hints in III, 1 (1046-48) of the traditional reconciliation when the miser quickly forgives his son for his earlier attempt to borrow money, but Molière otherwise departs from convention: a scene of reunion becomes the object of an elaborate parody in IV, 5 and, as has been seen already, any suggestion of harmony and forgiveness is left conspicuously absent in the denouement. The influence of Harpagon is seen indeed to permeate all who surround him, and the lovers tend to lack those characteristics traditionally associated with the young. The freshness, spontaneity or naïve charm found, for instance, in *La Princesse d'Elide*, *Le Bourgeois gentilhomme*, and *Le Malade imaginaire* are tinged here with other qualities: Cléante has a certain selfish impetuosity, irritated by talk of modesty and patience, complaining at 'les fâcheux sentiments d'un rigoureux honneur' (1506-07) or 'scrupuleuse bienséance' (1507); Valère a fierce sense of pride sensitive to 'soupçon outrageux' (30) from either Elise or Harpagon, and Elise's own affection cannot completely eradicate suspicion and mistrust:

> Ah! Valère, chacun tient les mêmes discours. Tous les hommes sont semblables par les paroles, et ce n'est que les actions qui les découvrent différents. (23-25)

This unusually prominent influence of the miser is suggested also by the absence in the comedy of a *raisonneur*, that figure who, in different ways, often serves to penetrate and control the absurdity of the central character. The spontaneous and stinging assessment of Philinte to Alceste in *Le Misanthrope* I, 1:

> Je vous dirai tout franc que cette maladie,
> Partout où vous allez, donne la comédie,

implies a stable comic perspective on the hero; a similar analysis of Harpagon by Maître Jacques has a more complex force. He, unlike the enlightened commentators in other comedies, is not detached from the obsession, but reflects and endorses it through his own proudly fulfilled double role as cook and groom. Indeed, the servants in *L'Avare* are quite different from those in other of Molière's comedies who outwit the protagonist or who refuse to take him seriously. In *Tartuffe*, Dorine manipulates Orgon with great success; in *Le Bourgeois gentilhomme* III, 2 Nicole controls Monsieur Jourdain by openly commenting on his ridiculousness ('vous êtes si plaisant, que je ne saurais me tenir de rire'); and in *Le Malade imaginaire* I, 5 Toinette characterises thus her important comic function:

> Quand un maître ne songe pas à ce qu'il fait, une servante

bien sensée est en droit de le redresser.

In *L'Avare*, no character consistently has the better of Harpagon, none has the articulate assurance to keep him in check; as a consequence the miser is not openly conceived of as an entertaining fool, rendered harmless by the firm control of normality. In *Le Bourgeois gentilhomme* V, 2 Dorante can speak confidently of the madness of M. Jourdain in a way which finds no echo in *L'Avare*:

> Oui, Madame, vous verrez la plus plaisante chose qu'on puisse voir; et je ne crois pas que dans tout le monde il soit possible de trouver encore un homme aussi fou que celui-là!

Further differences are apparent in the presentation of the central *imaginaire* himself. Immediately striking, for instance, is the total absence of feeling for his children — other fathers in Molière may well be tyrannical, but it is often a struggle. As Orgon menaces his daughter in *Tartuffe* IV, 3 he tries to overcome natural tenderness in a telling parody of the Cornelian hero ('Allons, ferme, mon cœur, point de faiblesse humaine', 1293) and having threatened to beat Louison, Argan, *le malade imaginaire*, is left distraught when he is taken in by her pretence of being dead (II, 8):

> Ah! ma fille! Ah! malheureux; ma pauvre fille est morte. Qu'ai-je fait, misérable? Ah! Chiennes de verges. La peste soit des verges! Ah! ma pauvre fille, ma pauvre petite Louison.

This is not the case with Harpagon. No parental affection conflicts with his unremitting avarice, and the life of his daughter is of far less interest to him than his wealth — for the miser, the fact that Valère once saved Elise from drowning in no way compensates him for the loss of his *cassette*:

> Tout cela n'est rien, et il valait bien mieux pour moi qu'il te

laissât noyer que de faire ce qu'il a fait. (2097-98)

The most significant difference of all, however, lies in the miser's attitude to others. It is something of a moral commonplace that the fool believes himself to be the only sane man, as Boileau observes in Satire IV:

> D'où vient, cher Le Vayer, que l'Homme le moins sage
> Croit toujours seul avoir la sagesse en partage:
> Et qu'il n'est point de Fou, qui par belles raisons
> Ne loge son voisin aux Petites-Maisons?

and when confronted with mockery, many of Molière's *obsédés* respond with confidence in themselves: in *M. de Pourceaugnac* the vain hero openly flouts 'la sotte ville, et les sottes gens qui y sont!' (I, 3), and in *Tartuffe* (III, 7) Orgon clearly delights in defying others: 'Faire enrager le monde est ma plus grande joie' (1173). However, whereas such characters scorn the world outside, Harpagon is afraid of it. In these other comedies the comic conflict is one between eloquent normality and self-assured absurdity; in *L'Avare* the tension originates more obviously within the miser himself and extends in different ways to those around him.

In this comedy, Molière goes further than anywhere else perhaps, in suggesting the powerful force of a passion which feeds on itself and can sap the very roots of normality. And yet the play is comic, not simply because it may amuse an audience, but in the very perspective which it offers. Stylisation of action and character, language and gesture ensure that emotional detachment which is the necessary precondition not just for laughter but also for a more lucid understanding of the play's subject in all its implications. In his *Critique de l'Ecole des femmes*, Sc. 5, Molière praised those who left all prejudice and emotion behind when they came to see his work performed, and who were able to judge:

> . . . par la bonne façon d'en juger, qui est de se laisser
> prendre aux choses, et de n'avoir ni prévention aveugle, ni

complaisance affectée, ni délicatesse ridicule.

It is from this standpoint, indeed, that the audience is in a position to perceive the discrepancies on which the comic vision is founded. In its highlighting of contrasts between young and old, guile and gullibility, normality and abnormality in language and behaviour, the comedy permits the spectator to suspend otherwise instinctive responses of terror, horror or pity in the face of domestic conflict; in its uncovering of tensions within Harpagon himself between confidence and suspicion, vanity and fear, it allows insight into the nature of an obsession, uncluttered by oversimple moral judgements; and, most revealing of all, in its juxtaposition of traditional elements and deviations from them it draws to the audience's attention the very artifice of comedy and underlines the complexity of the human affairs which it sets out to portray. The result is a comedy of avarice not limited to a particular time or reflecting a particular outlook, but which remains for audiences now, as in Molière's time, at once a delight and a challenge.

Select Bibliography

A. EDITIONS

1. *Œuvres complètes*, ed. G. Couton, Bibliothèque de la Pléiade, 2 vols, Paris: Gallimard, 1971.
2. *L'Avare*, ed. F. Angué, Univers des Lettres Bordas, Paris: Bordas, 1979.
3. *L'Avare*, ed. R.A. Wilson, Harrap's French Classics, London: Harrap, 1979.
4. *L'Avare*, ed. Ch. Dullin, Coll. Mises en Scène, Paris: Seuil, 1946.

B. OTHER WORKS CONTAINING STUDIES OF MISERS

5. Boileau, N. *Œuvres complètes*, ed. F. Escal, Bibliothèque de la Pléiade, Paris: Gallimard, 1966.
6. Boisrobert, F. de. *La Belle Plaideuse* (1654), ed. E. Fournier, in *Le Théâtre français au XVIe et au XVIIe siècle: choix des comédies les plus curieuses antérieures à Molière*, Paris: Laplace, Sanchez, 1871, pp.553-82.
7. Chappuzeau, S. *La Dame d'intrigue, ou le Riche Vilain* (1663), ed. V. Fournel, in *Les Contemporains de Molière: recueil de comédies rares ou peu connues jouées de 1650 à 1680*, 3 vols, Paris: Firmin Didot, 1863-75, I, 363-400.
8. Donneau de Visé, J. *La Mère coquette, ou les Amans brouillez* (1666), in *Théâtre françois, ou Recueil des meilleures pièces de théâtre*, 12 vols, Paris: Gandouin, 1737, VIII, 249-337.
9. La Bruyère, J. de. *Les Caractères*, ed. R. Garapon, Paris: Garnier, 1962.
10. La Fontaine, J. de. *Fables*, ed. G. Couton, Paris: Garnier, 1962.
11. Larivey, P. *Les Esprits* (1579), ed. M.J. Freeman, Textes Littéraires, 30, University of Exeter, 1978.
12. Tallemant des Réaux, G. *Historiettes*, ed. A. Adam, Bibliothèque de la Pléiade, 2 vols, Paris: Gallimard, 1960-61.

C. GENERAL AND BACKGROUND STUDIES BEFORE 1900

13. Fénelon, F. *Lettre à l'Académie* (1716), ed. E. Caldarini, Textes Littéraires Français, Geneva: Droz, 1970.
14. Grimarest, J. -L. de. *La Vie de M. de Molière* (1705), ed. G. Mongrédien, Paris: Brient, 1955.
15. Mongrédien, G. (ed.) *Recueil des textes et des documents du XVIIe siècle relatifs à Molière*, 2 vols, Paris: C.N.R.S., 1965.
16. Rapin, R. *Réflexions sur la poétique de ce temps et sur les ouvrages des poètes anciens et modernes* (1675), ed. E.T. Dubois, Geneva: Droz, 1970.

17. Riccoboni, L. *Observations sur la comédie et sur le génie de Molière*, Paris: Vve Pissot, 1736.

18. Rousseau, J.-J. *Lettre à M. d'Alembert sur les spectacles* (1758), ed. M. Fuchs, Textes Littéraires Français, Geneva: Droz, 1948.

19. Sarcey, F. *Quarante ans de théâtre*, 7 vols, Paris: Bibliothèque des Annales, 1900.

D. GENERAL AND BACKGROUND STUDIES AFTER 1900

20. Adam, A. *Histoire de la littérature française au XVIIe siècle*, 5 vols, Paris: del Duca, 1962-68.

21. Attinger, G. *L'Esprit de la commedia dell'arte dans le théâtre français*, Paris: Librairie Théâtrale, 1950.

22. Defaux, G. *Molière, ou les métamorphoses du comique: de la comédie morale au triomphe de la folie*, Lexington: French Forum, 1980.

23. Descotes, M. *Les Grands Rôles du théâtre de Molière*, Paris: P.U.F., 1960.

24. Eustis, A. *Molière as Ironic Contemplator*, The Hague: Mouton, 1973.

25. Fernandez, R. *Molière, ou l'essence du génie comique*, Paris: Grasset, 1979.

26. Gaxotte, P. *Molière*, Paris: Flammarion, 1977.

27. Hall, H.G. *Comedy in Context: essays on Molière*, Mississippi University Press, 1984.

28. Howarth, W.D. *Molière: a playwright and his audience*, Cambridge: C.U.P., 1982.

29. Knutson, H. *Molière: an archetypal approach*, Toronto University Press, 1976.

30. Moore, W.G. *Molière: a new criticism*, Oxford: Clarendon Press, 1949.

31. Simon, A. *Molière par lui-même*, Coll. Ecrivains de Toujours, Paris: Le Seuil, 1960.

32. Voltz, P. *La Comédie*, Coll. U. Série 'Lettres Françaises', Paris: A. Colin, 1964.

E. STUDIES SPECIFICALLY ON L'AVARE

33. Albanese, R. 'Argent et réification dans *L'Avare*', *Esprit Créateur* 21 (1981), 35-50.

34. Alsip, B.W. '*L'Avare*: history of scholarship', *Œuvres et Critiques*, 6 (1981), 99-110.

35. Arnavon, J. *Notes sur l'interprétation de Molière*, Paris: Plon, 1923.

36. Dauvin, S. & J. *L'Avare*, Profil d'une œuvre, 69, Paris: Hatier, 1979.

37. Dickson, J. '*L'Avare*: le rire et le jeu de l'inconséquence', *French Forum*, 5 (1980), 195-206.

38. Doolittle, J. 'Bad writing in *L'Avare*', *Esprit Créateur*, 6 (1966), 197-206.

39. Drysdall, D.L. '*L'Avare* and 'disconvenance'', *New Zealand Journal of French Studies*, 2 (1981), 5-33.

40. Dutton, R.R. *A Problem Play: Molière's 'L'Avare'*, French
     Monographs (Macquarie University) 2: 7, Jan. 1975.
41. Goode, W.O. 'The comic recognition scenes in *L'Avare*', *Romance
     Notes*, 14 (1972), 122-27.
42. Görschen, F. 'Die Geizkomödie im französischen Schriftum',
     Germanisch-Romanische Monatsschrift, 25 (1937), 207-24.
43. Gutwirth, M. 'The unity of Molière's *L'Avare*', *P.M.L.A.*, 76 (1961),
     359-66
44. Hubert, J.D. 'Theme and structure in *L'Avare*', *P.M.L.A.*, 75 (1960),
     31-36.
45. McBride, R. 'Harpagon ou le comédien comique' in *Humanitas:
     studies in French literature presented to Henri Godin*, ed. R.L. Davis
     et al., Coleraine: New University of Ulster, 1984, pp.49-64.
46. Peacock, N.A. 'The first two scenes of *L'Avare*: the aesthetic of
     illusion', *Quinquereme*, 8 (1985), 27-36.
47. Shaw, D. 'Harpagon's monologue', *Nottingham French Studies*, 23
     (1984), 1-11.
48. Walker, H. 'Action and ending of *L'Avare*', *French Review*, 34
     (1960-61), 531-36.
49. Zilly, B. *Molières 'L'Avare': die Struktur der Konflikte – zur Kritik
     der bürgerlichen Gesellschaft im 17ten Jahrhundert*, Romanistik, 14,
     Rheinfelden: Schäuble Verlag, 1979.

Bibliographical Supplement

EDITIONS

50. *L'Avare*. Préface de R. Planchon. Commentaires et notes de J. Morel,
     Le Livre de Poche, Paris: Librairie générale française, 1986.

STUDIES

51. Jones, D.F. 'The Treasure in the garden. Biblical imagery in
     L'Avare', *Papers on French Seventeenth-Century Literature*, 15
     (1988), 517-28.
52. Mallinson, G.J. 'Planchon's *L'Avare* and the expectations of a
     comedy', *French Studies Bulletin*, 23 (1987), 18-20.
53. Montbertrand, G. 'Territoire et société dans *l'Avare* et *Tartuffe* de
     Molière', *Theater and Society in French Literature*, French Literature
     Series, 15 (University of S. Carolina, 1988), 7-17.

54. Pineau, J. 'Harpagon ou la terre aride', *Revue d'Histoire du Théâtre*, 38 (1986), 406-17.
55. Powell, J. 'Making Faces. Character and physiognomy in *L'Ecole des Femmes* and *L'Avare*', *Seventeenth-Century French Studies*, 9 (1987), 94-112.
56. Sénart, P. '*L'Avare* d'après Roger Planchon (Théâtre Mogador)', *Revue des deux mondes* (janvier-mars 1987), 742-44.
57. Sweetser, M-O. '*Docere et delectare*: Richesses de *l'Avare*' in *Convergences: Rhetoric and Poetic in Seventeenth-Century France. Essays for Hugh M. Davidson*, ed. D.L. Rubin and M.B. McKinley (Columbus: Ohio State U.P., 1989), pp.110-20.

CRITICAL GUIDES TO FRENCH TEXTS

edited by
Roger Little, Wolfgang van Emden, David Williams